MASTER MOUNTAIN BIKING

A Complete Guide to Mountain Bike Skills, Trails, Gear, Fitness and Bike Repair for Thrilling Off-Road Adventures

J.J. Quest

This publication is designed to provide competent and reliable information regarding the subject matter covered. The material contained within this book is for informational purposes only. It is not intended to provide legal, medical, financial or other professional advice. Laws and practices often vary from state to state and country to country. If legal advice or other expert assistance is required, the services of a professional should be sought. The author and publisher specifically disclaim any liability that is incurred from the use or application of the contents of this book.

First Edition: September 2024

ISBN: 9798339502791

Contents

Dedication   1

Welcome to the World of Mountain Biking   2

   Beginner Fundamentals

   Skills Enhancement

   Maintenance and Repairs

   Trail Selection

   Safety and Gear

   Fitness and Training

   Community and Culture

   Final Thoughts

Section 1

   Mastering the Basics   12

   1. Essential Gear   15

   2. Bike Selection and Setup   19

   3. Handling Skills and Techniques   26

   4. Developing Balance and Control   31

   5. Recommended Maintenance and Repairs   35

   6. How To Maintain Your Bike   39

   7. Repairing Your Bike   43

   8. Finding the Best Trails to Start With   48

9. Trails for Building your Skills   51

10. The Best Apps and Devices for Mountain Biking   54

11. Essential Protective Gear   59

12. Riding Safely   64

13. Gear Checklist   68

14. Fitness and Training   73

15. Creating a Training Plan   77

16. Fueling Your Body   81

17. Finding People to Ride With   88

18. Participating in Events and Races   93

19. Supporting the Sport of Mountain Biking   98

Section 2

Evolving Your Riding Experience   104

20. Intermediate Skill Development and Riding Tech-   106
    niques

21. Advanced Skills and Techniques   111

22. Seasonal Riding Tips   118

23. Women-Specific Riding Tips   125

24. Youth and Family Biking   134

25. First Aid and Safety   143

26. Traveling with Your Bike   151

27. Biking Adventures   159

28. Epic Places to Ride   164

29. Staying Up with the Latest Trends and Advancements   170

Section 3

All About Electric Assist Mountain Biking on e-MTBs   176

30. Introduction to e-MTBs   181

31. Purchasing Guidance   187

32. All About e-MTB Batteries   193

33. Maximizing Your Battery's Lifespan   198

34. e-MTB Legal Regulations   203

35. e-MTB Trail Access   208

36. Important Riding Techniques for e-MTB Riders   213

37. Tips for Riding eMTB's on Various Terrains   219

38. eMTB Maintenance and Repair Basics   224

39. Troubleshooting Common e-MTB Issues   230

40. Maintaining and Repairing your e-MTB   236

41. Improving Your Fitness with an e-MTB   245

42. Health Benefits with e-MTB's over Traditional Bikes   250

43. Cool Features Available on e-MTBs   256

44. Integrating your e-MTB with Cycling Apps and other Digital Tools   263

45. Contributing to Sustainability   269

46. Environmental Considerations When Riding eMTBs   275

47. Connecting with Other e-MTB Riders   281

48. Events and Races for e-MTBs   288

49. Trail Maintenance and Advocacy   295

Now It is Time For You To Get Out There On Your Bike!   304

Reflecting on Your Progress

Embracing the Journey

Real-Life Inspirations

Your Path Forward

Final, Final, Thoughts

About the Author   310

Please Tell Us What You Think

Thank You for Your Support

This book is dedicated to my family with deep gratitude for all of our mountain biking adventures.

I'll always cherish the smiles and comments from those we passed on the trail—all six of us—when you were young. One of us leading the way, followed by four little duckies in a line, and the other riding sweep.

I'll never forget riding uphill with a super talkative kid on the trail-a-bike attached to my mountain bike, or the time one of us got stuck upside down between two trees after crashing to avoid running over a little ducky who had stopped suddenly in the middle of the trail.

From everyone lining up for basic bike maintenance—brakes working, tires pumped up—to our camping trips and biking singletrack at the UC, and catching air together at the bike park, these memories are the best of my life.

My hope is that you'll continue riding as adults and someday tell your own kids fond stories about mountain biking with your mom and dad.

I love you!

Welcome to the World of Mountain Biking

If you find yourself pondering questions related to mountain biking, such as where to begin, how to enhance your skills, maintain your bike, select trails, ensure safety, improve fitness, or connect with the community, then you are holding the right book. We even have an extensive bonus section that covers everything you could want to know about mountain biking with e-MTB's! This guide is tailored to address these essential areas, providing you with the knowledge and confidence to embark on your mountain biking journey.

Mountain biking is an exhilarating outdoor sport that combines the thrill of off-road cycling with the challenge of navigating diverse terrains. Whether you're interested in cross-country adventures, downhill descents, or tackling singletrack trails, this book covers all aspects of the sport. With chapters on biking gear, bike maintenance, cycling techniques, and bike repair, you'll have everything you need to keep your bike in top condition and enhance your riding ability.

This guide also dives into trail selection, helping you find the best mountain bike parks and mountain bike trails for every skill level, from beginner to advanced. Whether you're seeking the excitement of mountain bike racing, the endurance challenge of bikepacking, or the joy of trail riding, you'll find valuable insights here. We'll discuss bike safety to ensure every adventure is enjoyable and safe, and provide fitness and training tips for building the strength and endurance needed for mountain biking.

Furthermore, this guide will help you connect with the vibrant mountain biking community and culture. Engaging with local groups, attending mountain biking events, and participating in community efforts like trail maintenance and advocacy will enrich your experience and foster a deeper connection to the sport.

Mountain biking is not just about riding; it is an adventure that encompasses bike maintenance, exploring scenic trails, honing mountain bike skills, and embracing the culture of outdoor sports. As you delve into this guide, you'll discover important insights that will help you become a competent and confident rider. Let's explore each key area of interest to understand why they are critical for both newcomers and seasoned riders alike.

Beginner Fundamentals

Embarking on any new sport can be daunting, and mountain biking is no exception. As a newcomer, understanding the basic fundamentals sets a solid foundation for your journey. This section is crucial because it demystifies the sport, breaking it down into manageable steps.

Why It's Important

Trust and Confidence: Starting with the right knowledge builds confidence. When you know the essential gear, basic riding techniques, and trail etiquette, you'll feel more comfortable and prepared.

Safety: Understanding the basics helps prevent injuries. Knowing how to properly fit a helmet, choose the right bike, and maintain correct posture on the bike are fundamental safety measures.

Common Concerns

What gear do I need? Many beginners are unsure about the essential gear required to start. From helmets and gloves to the right bike, knowing what to invest in first can be overwhelming.

How do I choose and set up my bike? Selecting the right bike and setting it up properly is crucial for comfort and performance. Questions about bike types, sizes, and initial adjustments are common.

Am I ready for mountain biking? Concerns about physical readiness and skill level often cross the minds of newcomers. Understanding that there are trails and riding styles suited for all levels ensures that everyone can start at their pace.

Skills Enhancement

Once you've mastered the basics, the next step is to enhance your riding skills. Improving your mountain bike skills not only helps you tackle more challenging trails but also increases your overall enjoyment and safety.

Why It's Important

Progression: Skill enhancement is crucial for progressing in any sport. It helps you tackle more complex trails with confidence and competence.

Safety: Advanced skills reduce the risk of falls and injuries. Techniques like proper braking, cornering, and descending are essential for navigating difficult terrains safely.

Enjoyment: As your skills improve, so does your enjoyment. Challenging yourself with new mountain bike trails and techniques keeps the sport exciting and fulfilling.

Common Concerns

How do I climb steep tracks efficiently? Many riders struggle with climbing. Techniques to conserve energy and maintain traction are frequently sought after.

How do I handle technical descents? Descending can be intimidating. Riders often seek advice on maintaining control and balance during steep or technical descents.

What drills can improve my handling skills? Advanced handling skills, like cornering and jumping, are areas where riders look for specific drills and practice routines.

Maintenance and Repairs

Keeping your mountain bike in top condition is essential for performance and safety. Regular maintenance and knowing how to perform basic repairs can prevent unexpected breakdowns and prolong the life of your bike.

Why It's Important

Reliability: A well-maintained bike is more reliable and less likely to experience mechanical failures on the trail.

Safety: Proper maintenance ensures that your bike functions safely. Braking components, for example, must be routinely checked and adjusted to prevent accidents.

Cost-Effective: Regular maintenance and basic bike repair can save you money in the long run by preventing more serious damage that requires costly professional repairs.

Common Concerns

How often should I service my bike? Riders often wonder about the frequency and scope of maintenance tasks.

What tools do I need for basic repairs? Understanding the essential tools for at-home maintenance and trailside repairs is a common concern.

How do I fix a flat tire or broken chain on the trail? Knowing how to address common mechanical issues on the trail is crucial for uninterrupted riding.

Trail Selection

Finding the best places to ride is vital for a safe and enjoyable mountain biking experience. Whether you're looking for beginner-friendly trails or more challenging terrains, understanding trail selection is essential.

Why It's Important

Matching Skill Level: Choosing trails that match your skill level ensures that you are not overwhelmed and can ride safely.

Exploration: Knowing where to find new trails keeps your rides exciting and varied. It allows you to explore new areas and experience different types of terrain.

Safety: Understanding trail conditions and difficulty prevents you from attempting trails that are beyond your capability, reducing the risk of accidents.

Common Concerns

What are the best beginner-friendly trails in my area? Beginners often seek recommendations for trails that are suitable for their skill level.

How do I find trails that match my abilities? Riders look for tools and resources to help them identify trails that provide the right level of challenge.

What resources are best for trail maps and navigation? Navigating unfamiliar trails requires reliable maps and tools, which can be a concern for many riders.

Safety and Gear

Ensuring a safe and enjoyable ride involves using the right gear and following safety practices. This area covers everything from protective gear to riding techniques that enhance safety.

Why It's Important

Protection: The right gear can prevent injuries. Helmets, pads, and proper clothing are essential for protection.

Confidence: Knowing you're equipped with the right safety gear boosts your confidence on the trail.

Preparedness: Safety extends beyond protective gear to include tools and knowledge for handling emergencies and repairs.

Common Concerns

What protective gear do I need? Riders often want to know the essential safety gear they should invest in.

How can I prevent injuries while riding? Techniques and habits that reduce the risk of injuries are a major concern for many.

What should I pack for a day of mountain biking? Understanding what to carry for a safe and prepared ride is crucial, especially for longer outings.

Fitness and Training

Improving your physical performance for riding is key for endurance, strength, and overall riding efficiency. Fitness and training are integral parts of becoming a better mountain biker.

Why It's Important

Endurance: Good fitness levels allow you to ride longer and with more energy. It's crucial for tackling more extended trails and steep climbs.

Strength: Building muscle strength improves your control over the bike, making it easier to handle difficult terrains.

Health: Regular training ensures that you are fit and healthy, reducing the chance of injuries and improving overall well-being.

Common Concerns

What exercises improve my strength and endurance? Riders look for specific workouts that target the muscles used in mountain biking.

How can I create a training plan that fits my schedule? Balancing training with other life commitments is a common challenge.

What nutrition tips should I follow for mountain biking? Proper nutrition is essential for sustained energy and recovery, making it a vital concern for riders.

Community and Culture

Engaging with the mountain biking community enriches your experience. Joining groups, participating in events, and supporting trail maintenance all form a part of community engagement.

Why It's Important

Support and Learning: Joining a community provides support and opportunities to learn from experienced riders.

Camaraderie: Being part of a like-minded community enhances enjoyment and provides motivation.

Advocacy and Sustainability: Contributing to trail maintenance and advocacy efforts ensures the sustainability of the sport and the trails we cherish.

Common Concerns

How can I connect with local mountain biking groups or clubs? Finding and joining local groups is a concern for many riders looking to connect.

What are popular mountain biking events or races? Riders seek information on events that provide both challenges and community engagement.

How can I support trail maintenance and advocacy efforts? Many riders are keen to give back to the community and support the upkeep of trails.

Final Thoughts

As you ponder these pivotal questions about mountain biking—whether you are concerned with getting started, improving your skills, maintaining your bike, selecting the best trails, ensuring safety, enhancing your fitness, or engaging with the community—you've chosen the right book. Each of these areas is critical to your development as a mountain biker and to enjoying this exhilarating sport to its fullest.

This comprehensive guide is designed to address each of these key areas with detailed, experienced, and easy-to-understand advice. Embrace the journey, and let's hit the trails together!

Enjoyment: A solid grasp of the fundamentals enhances your enjoyment. With the right start, you'll find more joy and less frustration on the trails.

Section One
Mastering the Basics

Mastering the Basics

Mountain biking can bring you so much fun, adventure and just pure joy. There is something about whizzing down a trail in the woods that you won't understand until you do it. So lets get you started on the right foot so that you fall in love with mountain biking like we have. Remember, no matter what, having fun, learning new skills, challenging yourself gently and just getting out there (even if you are walking your bike up or down half the trail) is the goal.

Here Is What We Cover In Section One

Getting Started

- What are the essential pieces of gear I need to start mountain biking?

- How do I choose and set up my bike?

Skills Enhancement

- How can I improve my balance and control on technical trails?

- What are the basic techniques for handling a mountain bike on different terrains?

Maintenance and Repairs

- How often should I service my mountain bike?

- What are the common bike maintenance tasks I can do myself?

- How do I repair a flat tire or fix a broken chain on the trail?

Trail Selection and Navigation

- What are some of the best beginner-friendly trails in my area?

- How can I find and choose trails that match my skill level?

- What are the best resources for trail maps and navigation?

Safety and Gear

- What protective gear is essential for mountain biking?

- How can I prevent injuries while riding?

- What should I pack for a day of mountain biking?

Fitness and Training

- What exercises can I do to improve my strength and endurance for mountain biking?

- How can I create a training plan that fits my schedule?

- What nutrition tips should I follow to fuel my mountain biking adventures?

Community and Culture

- How can I connect with local mountain biking groups or clubs?

- What are some popular mountain biking events or races I can participate in?

- How can I contribute to and support trail maintenance and advocacy efforts?

- How can I stay up-to-date with the latest trends and advancements in mountain biking?

CHAPTER 1

Essential Gear

What are the essential pieces of gear I need to start mountain biking?

Starting mountain biking requires the right gear to ensure safety, comfort, and enjoyment. While mountain biking can be gear-intensive, beginners can start with a few essentials before gradually expanding their collection. Here's a comprehensive guide to the must-have gear for new mountain bikers:

Essential Gear

Mountain Bike

Types: There are several types of mountain bikes, including cross-country, trail, enduro, and downhill. As a beginner, a trail bike is a versatile choice that can handle a variety of terrains.

Example: The Trek Marlin 7 is a popular entry-level trail bike known for its reliability and performance.

Key Features: Look for features like front suspension (hardtail), disc brakes, and a durable frame. Full-suspension bikes offer more comfort but can be pricier.

Helmet

Importance: Head protection is non-negotiable. A good helmet can prevent serious injuries.

Types: Choose between half-shell helmets for general riding and full-face helmets for downhill or more aggressive trails.

Example: The Bell Super 3R MIPS offers a removable chin bar, making it versatile for both trail and downhill riding.

Fit and Comfort: Ensure the helmet fits snugly but comfortably, with adequate ventilation and safety certifications (e.g., MIPS technology).

Protective Gear

Gloves: Padded gloves protect your hands from blisters, impacts, and improve grip.

Knee and Elbow Pads: Essential for aggressive trails or downhill riding.

Example: Fox Racing Ranger gloves and G-Form Pro-X knee and elbow pads are well-regarded for comfort and protection.

Apparel

Jersey and Shorts: Wear moisture-wicking, breathable materials. Padded shorts enhance comfort on long rides.

Shoes: Flat shoes with good grip are suitable for beginners. Once confident, clipless shoes (with cleats) can improve pedaling efficiency.

Example: Five Ten Freerider shoes are popular for their grip on flat pedals.

Hydration and Nutrition

Hydration Pack: A backpack with a water reservoir (e.g., CamelBak) keeps you hydrated on long rides.

Water Bottle: For shorter rides, a water bottle and cage attached to your bike frame suffice.

Snacks: Carry energy bars, gels, or snacks to maintain energy levels.

Basic Tools and Repair Kit

Multitool: A compact multitool with Allen wrenches, screwdrivers, and a chain tool.

Pump/Tire Inflator: A portable pump or CO_2 inflator for quick tire fixes.

Tube and Patch Kit: Spare inner tube and patch kit for puncture repairs.

Example: The Topeak Alien II multitool and Lezyne Sport Drive HV pump are reliable choices.

Eye Protection

Sunglasses or Goggles: Protects your eyes from debris, UV rays, and glare.

Example: Oakley Radar EV sunglasses provide excellent clarity and protection.

Lighting (if riding in low light)

Front and Rear Lights: Ensure visibility and safety during dawn, dusk, or night rides.

Example: The Cygolite Metro Pro 1100 front light and Hotshot Pro rear light are robust and bright options.

Additional Tips for Beginners

Rent or Borrow Gear: If you're unsure about the sport, consider renting a bike or borrowing gear to get a feel for it before investing.

Join a Local Club: Many biking clubs offer beginner rides and can provide valuable advice on essential gear tailored to your local terrain.

Visit a Specialized Bike Shop: Staff can offer personalized recommendations based on your body size, riding style, and budget.

Final Thoughts

Investing in the right gear not only enhances your mountain biking experience but also ensures you stay safe and comfortable on the trails. As you progress and ride more frequently, you can gradually add more specialized equipment to your collection. But for now, focus on getting the basics right, and enjoy the thrill of your new adventure!

CHAPTER 2

Bike Selection and Setup

How do I choose and set up my bike?

Choosing and setting up your mountain bike properly is crucial for ensuring a comfortable, safe, and enjoyable riding experience. Whether you're a beginner or an experienced rider, understanding the key aspects of selecting and configuring your bike will help you make the most of your mountain biking adventures. Here's an in-depth guide to help you choose and set up your mountain bike.

Understanding Different Types of Mountain Bikes

Cross-Country (XC) Bikes

Description: Designed for speed and efficiency on varied terrain. Typically lighter with less suspension travel (80-120mm).

Ideal For: Long-distance rides, climbs, and moderate trails.

Example: The Specialized Epic is a popular XC bike known for its lightweight and efficient design.

Trail Bikes

Description: Versatile bikes suitable for a wide range of terrains. Feature moderate suspension travel (120-150mm) and balanced geometry.

Ideal For: General trail riding, varied terrain, and moderate technical features.

Example: The Trek Fuel EX is a renowned trail bike offering a good balance of performance and comfort.

All-Mountain/Enduro Bikes

Description: Robust bikes designed for challenging technical descents and climbs. Have more suspension travel (150-170mm) and aggressive geometry.

Ideal For: Technical trails, steep descents, and aggressive riding.

Example: The Santa Cruz Nomad is a favored choice for enduro racing and aggressive trail riding.

Downhill (DH) Bikes

Description: Built for extreme descents and rough terrain. Feature extensive suspension travel (170-200mm) and slack geometry.

Ideal For: Downhill racing, bike parks, and very technical descents.

Example: The Canyon Sender is a top-rated downhill bike known for its stability and performance on steep descents.

Fat Bikes

Description: Feature oversized tires (3.8 inches or wider) for riding on soft surfaces like snow or sand.

Ideal For: Snowy, sandy, or muddy conditions where traction is key.

Example: The Salsa Mukluk is a recognized fat bike suitable for all-season adventures.

Finding the Perfect Trail Bike

Jessica, a new mountain biking enthusiast, decided to invest in her first trail bike. She researched different types of bikes and determined that a trail bike suited her needs for versatility. Jessica visited her local bike shop for a professional fitting, selecting a medium frame with 140mm of suspension travel. She opted for a 1x12 drivetrain for simplicity and hydraulic disc brakes for superior stopping power. With assistance from the shop, Jessica set up her bike's suspension, saddle, and handlebar positions perfectly. Her first ride on her new bike was comfortable, confident, and incredibly fun, affirming that she made the right choice through proper research and setup.

Choosing the Right Frame Size

Frame Size

Importance: Correct frame size ensures comfort, control, and efficiency.

How to Determine: Use the manufacturer's size chart based on your height and inseam measurement. Many bike shops offer professional fitting services.

Stand-over Height

Importance: Ensure there is adequate clearance (1-2 inches) between the top tube and your inseam when standing over the bike.

Example: Jill, who is 5'7", uses the size chart to select a medium frame, ensuring a comfortable and safe fit.

Suspension Type and Setup

Hardtail vs. Full Suspension

Hardtail: Features front suspension only; lighter and more efficient for climbs and less technical terrain.

Full Suspension: Features both front and rear suspension; provides more comfort and control on technical and rough terrain.

Example: Julie chooses a full suspension bike to minimize saddle fatigue and chaffing especially common for women on long, technical rides.

Suspension Travel

Importance: Choose based on the terrain you plan to ride. XC bikes have less travel (80-120mm), while downhill bikes have more (170-200mm).

Example: John chooses a trail bike with 140mm of travel for its versatility on varied terrain.

Component Selection

Drivetrain

Single vs. Multiple Chainrings: Single chainring setups (1x) are simpler and lighter, making them popular for modern mountain bikes.

Gear Range: Ensure a wide gear range to handle climbs and descents. An 11-speed or 12-speed cassette is common.

Example: Emily opts for a 1x12 drivetrain for simplicity and sufficient gear range on her trail rides.

Brakes

Disc Brakes: Hydraulic disc brakes offer superior stopping power and modulation compared to mechanical discs or rim brakes.

Example: Mike upgrades to hydraulic disc brakes for improved performance on technical descents.

Tires

Width and Tread: Choose wider tires (2.3-2.6 inches) for better traction and stability. Tread patterns should match the terrain you ride most frequently.

Example: Sarah selects wider, knobby tires for better grip on the rocky trails near her home.

Dropper Post

Description: A seat post that can be adjusted on the fly, lowering the saddle for descents and raising it for climbs.

Example: David installs a dropper post for more efficient transitions between descending and climbing so he does not overstrain his injured knee on steep ascents.

Setting Up Your Bike

Saddle Height and Position

Height: Adjust the saddle height so that your leg has a slight bend at the knee when the pedal is at the bottom of the stroke.

Position: Ensure the saddle is level and positioned correctly for comfort.

Example: Lisa adjusts her saddle height and fore-aft position to optimize her pedaling efficiency and comfort.

Handlebar and Stem

Handlebar Width: Choose a width that provides stability without compromising control.

Stem Length: A shorter stem can improve control on technical terrain, while a longer stem can enhance climbing efficiency.

Examples: Simon adjusts his handlebar width and replaces the stock stem with a shorter one for better control on technical descents. Emma replaces the stock stem with a taller one because a more upright position is more comfortable on her back and female parts.

Suspension Setup

Sag Measurement: Set the sag (compression of the suspension when seated) according to the manufacturer's recommendations, typically around 20-30% of the suspension's total travel.

Rebound and Compression: Fine-tune the rebound and compression settings based on your riding style and terrain.

Example: Mark sets his suspension sag and adjusts the rebound damping for his preferred balance of comfort and control on rough trails.

Brake and Shifter Position

Ergonomics: Position brake levers and shifters within easy reach while maintaining a comfortable grip on the handlebars.

Example: Tom adjusts his brake levers to a 45-degree angle, ensuring quick and comfortable access without straining his wrists.

Finding the Perfect Trail Bike

Jessica, a new mountain biking enthusiast, decided to invest in her first trail bike. She researched different types of bikes and determined that a trail bike suited her needs for versatility. Jessica visited her local bike shop for a professional fitting, selecting a medium frame with 140mm of suspension travel. She opted for a 1x12 drivetrain for simplicity and hydraulic disc brakes for superior stopping power. With assistance from the shop, Jessica set up her bike's suspension, saddle, and handlebar positions perfectly. Her first ride on her new bike was comfortable, confident, and incredibly fun, affirming that she made the right choice through proper research and setup.

Final Thoughts

Choosing and setting up your mountain bike properly is essential for a great riding experience. By understanding the different types of mountain bikes, selecting the right frame size and components, and setting up your bike to fit your body and riding style, you can ensure comfort, control, and enjoyment on the trails. Take the time to find the perfect bike and make necessary adjustments, and you'll be ready to tackle any adventure with confidence.

CHAPTER 3

Handling Skills and Techniques

What are the basic techniques for handling a mountain bike on different terrains?

Mastering basic mountain biking techniques is crucial for riding safely and confidently on various terrains. Here's a detailed guide to essential skills that will help you handle different trail conditions:

Body Position

Neutral Position

When to Use: Ideal for flat or less technical sections.

How to Perform: Keep your pedals level with one foot forward. Bend your elbows slightly, and keep your knees slightly bent. Your body should be relaxed but in control, with your weight evenly distributed.

Attack Position

When to Use: Used when approaching obstacles or technical sections.

How to Perform: Stand up on the pedals, maintaining a low center of gravity. Your elbows and knees should be bent more than in the neutral position, and your weight should be centered over the bike. Keep your eyes focused ahead to anticipate changes in the trail.

Cornering

Basic Technique

How to Perform: Enter the corner wide, adjust your speed before the turn, and lean your bike into the turn while keeping your body more upright. Look through the turn to where you want to go.

Body Position: Slightly shift your weight to the outside pedal and keep it down. Your inside hand should apply light pressure on the handlebars to guide the turn.

Advanced Tips

Trail Surface: On loose or muddy trails, avoid sharp braking while turning. Keep traction by maintaining a smooth, controlled speed.

Braking

Effective Braking

How to Perform: Use both brakes simultaneously but rely more on the front brake (approximately 70% front, 30% rear) for effective stopping power. Always brake before a corner, not during the turn.

Body Position: Shift your weight back slightly to prevent going over the handlebars and keep your body stable.

Terrain Considerations

Downhill: Modulate both brakes to control speed. Avoid locking your wheels.

Wet or Loose Terrain: Apply brakes gently and in a controlled manner to maintain traction.

Climbing

Basic Technique

How to Perform: Shift to a lower gear before the climb. Maintain a steady, moderate pace.

Body Position: Stay seated as much as possible to keep traction on the rear wheel. Lean slightly forward and keep your elbows and knees close to the bike.

Advanced Tips

Technical Climbs: When tackling steep or rocky climbs, shift your weight forward and pull up on the handlebars to maintain traction and control.

Descending

Basic Technique

How to Perform: Use a low gear and control your speed using both brakes.

Body Position: Stand on the pedals with knees and elbows bent. Shift your weight back and keep your heels dropped. Look ahead to choose your line.

Advanced Tips

Rough Terrain: Stay relaxed and let the bike move beneath you. Use your legs and arms as suspension to absorb impacts.

Steep Descents: Feather the brakes to control speed without skidding.

Navigating Obstacles

Basic Obstacles (Rocks, Roots)

How to Perform: Approach obstacles in a straight line. Use the attack position to stay balanced and absorb impacts.

Body Position: Keep your pedals level and allow the bike to roll over obstacles.

Advanced Obstacles (Drops, Jumps)

Drops: Shift your weight back and extend your arms and legs to absorb the drop. Practice on small drops before attempting larger ones.

Jumps: Approach with moderate speed. As your front wheel leaves the ground, pull up on the handlebars and use your legs to lift the rear wheel. Stay centered over the bike and land with your knees and elbows slightly bent to absorb the impact.

Sarah's First Technical Ride

Sarah, a novice mountain biker, decided to try a new trail with rocks and roots after mastering basic terrains. She started by practicing her body position on flat terrain. When approaching a rocky section, she used the attack position to maintain control. By applying the braking techniques she learned, Sarah effectively managed her speed downhill. Throughout her ride, she realized that looking ahead and anticipating obstacles greatly improved her confidence and control.

Final Thoughts

Mastering these basic mountain biking techniques will significantly enhance your riding experience, allowing you to tackle various terrains with confidence and efficiency. As you gain experience, continue to practice and refine these skills on different trails and conditions. Remember, mountain biking is as much about enjoying the journey as it is about perfecting your technique.

CHAPTER 4

Developing Balance and Control

How can I improve my balance and control on technical trails?

Improving balance and control on technical trails requires intentional practice and understanding of your bike's dynamics. Here are detailed steps and exercises that will help you enhance your skills:

Balance and Control Skills & Techniques

Riding Position

Neutral Position: Use this when riding on smoother, less technical sections. Keep your pedals level, with a slight bend in your knees and elbows. Your weight should be evenly distributed.

Attack Position: This is crucial for technical sections. Stand on your pedals, knees and elbows bent, with your weight centered over the bike. Your body should be relaxed but ready to react to the terrain.

Core Strength

Importance: A strong core stabilizes your body and improves bike handling.

Exercises: Incorporate planks, Russian twists, and leg raises into your fitness routine. These exercises target your core and enhance stability and control.

Track Stand Practice

How to Perform: Find a flat area. Stand on your pedals, keep your front wheel slightly turned, and use subtle motions to keep your balance without moving forward.

Benefits: This exercise improves your balance and control, especially useful for technical sections where you may need to pause and navigate carefully.

Slow Riding

How to Perform: Practice riding as slowly as possible without putting your foot down. Focus on smooth, controlled movements.

Benefits: Enhances your ability to maintain balance and control at low speeds, which is crucial for technical trails.

Weight Shifting

Front and Rear Shifting: Practice shifting your weight forward (climbs) and back (descents) to maintain traction and control.

Side to Side: On twisty or uneven trails, shifting your weight from side to side helps keep balance and enables smoother navigation around obstacles.

Use Your Knees and Elbows

Shock Absorbers: Think of your knees and elbows as shock absorbers. Keep them bent and flexible to absorb bumps and maintain control.

Example: When riding over roots and rocks, allow your bike to move beneath you, using your arms and legs to absorb the impact.

Pump Tracks and Skill Parks

Practice Grounds: Visit local pump tracks or skill parks. These areas offer safe environments to practice handling, balance, and control on rollers and berms.

Exercises: Ride the pump track without pedaling, using your body movements to gain and maintain speed. This teaches efficient weight shifting and balance.

Look Ahead

Importance: Always look ahead to where you want to go, not directly in front of your wheel. This helps anticipate and react to obstacles in advance.

Example: On technical descents, focus on the trail ahead to choose the best line and avoid unexpected hazards.

Tom's Improvement Story

Tom struggled with balance on technical trails. He dedicated time to practicing track stands and slow riding in his backyard. Gradually, he noticed significant improvement in his balance and control on the trail. By visiting a local pump track, he further enhanced his skills, especially on berms and rollers. This foundational practice made Tom more confident and capable on challenging trails.

Final Thoughts

Improving your balance and control on technical trails is a gradual process that combines practical exercises, strength training, and consistent practice. By focusing on these foundational techniques and regularly challenging yourself on various terrains, you'll become a more competent and confident rider. Remember, the goal is to ride smoothly and safely, making your mountain biking adventures even more enjoyable.

CHAPTER 5

Recommended Maintenance and Repairs

How often should I service my mountain bike?

Regular maintenance is key to keeping your mountain bike in top condition and ensuring a smooth and safe ride. Here's a comprehensive guide on how often you should service different parts of your bike:

Recommended Maintenance and Repair Schedule

Daily/Every Ride

Pre-Ride Check: Before every ride, perform a quick check:

Tires: Ensure they are properly inflated. Check for any cuts or debris.

Brakes: Test both front and rear brakes to make sure they function correctly.

Chain: Check that the chain is clean and properly lubricated.

Weekly/Bi-Weekly

Cleaning: Clean your bike thoroughly, especially after muddy or wet rides. Use a gentle bike-specific cleaner and a soft brush.

Lubrication: Lubricate the chain and other moving parts after cleaning. Clean off excess lubricant to avoid attracting dirt.

Inspection: Inspect the frame, fork, and components for any signs of wear or damage. Tighten loose bolts.

Monthly

Brake Pads and Cables: Check the brake pads for wear and replace them if they are worn down. Inspect brake cables for fraying or stretching.

Drivetrain: Inspect the drivetrain (chain, cassette, chainrings, and derailleur). Look for wear and ensure the shifting is smooth.

Wheel Check: Check the wheels for true (no wobbling) and ensure the spokes are tight.

Quarterly

Suspension: If you have a suspension fork or rear shock, check the air pressure and rebound settings. Clean and inspect the stanchions for scratches or dirt.

Headset and Bottom Bracket: Check for play or looseness. Tighten or adjust if necessary.

Bearings: Check wheel and hub bearings for smoothness. Service or replace if they feel rough.

Every Six Months

Full Tune-Up: A full tune-up includes adjusting brakes and shifting, truing wheels, checking the drivetrain, and ensuring all bolts are properly torqued.

Suspension Service: Depending on your usage, suspension components may need a more in-depth service, including oil changes and seal replacements.

Annually

Professional Service: Consider taking your bike to a professional mechanic for a thorough inspection and servicing. They can spot issues that may not be visible to the untrained eye.

Replace Consumable Parts: Replace frequently worn parts, such as the chain, cassette, and brake pads, to maintain optimal performance.

Emma's Regular Maintenance Routine

Emma rides her mountain bike several times a week. She carries out a pre-ride check before every ride, ensuring her tires are inflated and her brakes work properly. Once a week, she cleans her bike and lubricates the chain. Monthly, she inspects her brake pads and cables, and every six months, she performs a full tune-up. Annually, Emma takes her bike to a professional for a detailed inspection. This routine keeps her bike running smoothly and minimizes unexpected breakdowns.

Final Thoughts

Regular maintenance of your mountain bike not only prolongs its lifespan but also enhances your riding experience by preventing mechanical failures. Make a habit of performing routine checks and cleaning, and don't hesitate to consult a professional mechanic for more complex services. Your bike will thank you with reliable performance and countless enjoyable rides.

CHAPTER 6

How To Maintain Your Bike

What are the common bike maintenance tasks I can do myself?

Performing basic bike maintenance tasks yourself can save you time and money, and ensures your bike remains in optimal condition. Here are some common maintenance tasks that are simple enough to do at home:

Performing Basic Maintenance

Cleaning Your Bike

Importance: Regular cleaning avoids the buildup of dirt and grime, which can wear out components faster.

Tools Needed: Bike cleaner or mild soap, brushes (including an old toothbrush), sponge, water hose.

Steps: Rinse the bike with water. Apply cleaner to the frame, drivetrain, and other components. Scrub gently with brushes and sponge, then rinse off the soap. Dry with a clean cloth.

Example: After a muddy ride, cleaning ensures that mud and debris don't stick to moving parts, avoiding abrasive damage.

Lubricating the Chain

Importance: Keeps the chain running smoothly and prolongs its life.

Tools Needed: Bike-specific chain lubricant, rag.

Steps: Clean the chain with a rag if dirty. Apply a drop of lube to each link while turning the crank backward. Wipe off excess lube with a clean rag.

Tip: Avoid over-lubricating, as this attracts more dirt.

Checking and Inflating Tires

Importance: Proper tire pressure ensures better control and reduces the risk of flats.

Tools Needed: Tire pump with a pressure gauge.

Steps: Check the recommended pressure on the tire sidewall. Inflate the tires to the recommended PSI.

Tip: Check tire pressure before every ride.

Inspecting and Replacing Brake Pads

Importance: Ensures effective braking and safety.

Tools Needed: Allen wrench, new brake pads.

Steps: Inspect brake pads regularly. If they are worn down to the wear line, replace them. Use an Allen wrench to remove the old pads and install new ones.

Tip: Always replace pads in pairs to maintain balanced braking.

Adjusting Brake and Gear Cables

Importance: Ensures smooth braking and shifting.

Tools Needed: Allen wrench, cable cutters.

Steps: For brakes, adjust the tension by turning the barrel adjuster. For gears, fine-tune the derailleur using the barrel adjuster on the shifter.

Example: If your shifting becomes rough or inaccurate, a simple cable adjustment can restore smooth operation.

Truing Wheels

Importance: Keeps the wheels straight and aligned, preventing wobbling.

Tools Needed: Spoke wrench, truing stand (optional).

Steps: Identify wobbles by spinning the wheel and watching for side-to-side movement. Tighten or loosen spokes with a spoke wrench. If needed, use a truing stand for accuracy.

Tip: Make small adjustments to avoid over-tightening spokes.

Replacing a Chain

Importance: Essential if the chain is stretched or damaged.

Tools Needed: Chain tool, new chain, quick link (optional).

Steps: Use a chain wear indicator to check for stretch. Remove the old chain with a chain tool. Fit the new chain, matching the length of the old one, and connect it using a quick link or chain tool.

Example: Replacing a stretched chain prevents wear on other drivetrain components, saving you money in the long run.

Checking and Tightening Bolts

Importance: Prevents parts from loosening and ensures integrity.

Tools Needed: Allen wrench set, torque wrench (optional).

Steps: Regularly check bolts on the handlebars, stem, seat post, and other parts. Use the appropriate Allen wrench to tighten any loose bolts.

Tip: Use a torque wrench to tighten bolts to the manufacturer's specifications.

John's Weekend Maintenance Routine

Every weekend, John dedicates an hour to maintaining his mountain bike. He starts by cleaning it thoroughly, then lubricates the chain. He checks the tire pressure and inspects the brake pads and cables, adjusting them as needed. John also takes time to check and tighten bolts. This routine often only takes 15 minutes and it keeps his bike in excellent condition, ready for any trail adventure.

Final Thoughts

Performing these common maintenance tasks yourself ensures your mountain bike remains reliable and safe to ride. While some tasks may seem daunting at first, with practice, they become straightforward, empowering you to take better care of your bike. Regular maintenance not only enhances performance but also extends the lifespan of your equipment, making each ride more enjoyable.

Chapter 7

Repairing Your Bike

How do I repair a flat tire or fix a broken chain on the trail?

Knowing how to repair a flat tire or fix a broken chain on the trail can save your ride from being cut short. Here's a step-by-step guide to handling these common issues:

Basic Bike Repairs You Can Do Yourself

Repairing a Flat Tire

Tools Needed:

- Tire levers

- Spare tube or patch kit

- Pump or CO2 inflator

- Multi-tool (optional but often helpful)

Steps to Repair a Flat Tire:

1.Remove the Wheel

Shift to the smallest cog and chainring to make wheel removal easier.

Open the brake quick release (if applicable).

Use a quick release lever or axle nuts to remove the wheel from the frame.

2. Remove the Tire

Insert a tire lever under the bead of the tire (the edge of the tire that fits into the rim).

Pry the tire over the rim edge. Use a second tire lever if needed, moving around the tire until one side is off the rim.

3. Remove the Tube

Pull the tube out from between the tire and rim. Be careful around the valve stem.

If you're patching the tube, inflate it slightly and locate the puncture by feeling for air escaping or submerging the tube in water and looking for bubbles.

4. Patch the Tube (if applicable)

Roughen the area around the puncture with sandpaper (included in the patch kit).

Apply glue and wait a few minutes for it to become tacky.

Press the patch firmly over the puncture and hold it in place.

5. Install the New or Patched Tube

Lightly inflate the tube to give it shape.

Insert the tube back into the tire, starting with the valve stem through the rim hole.

Work the tube into the tire around the rim.

6. Reinstall the Tire

Use your hands to push the tire bead back onto the rim. Begin at the valve stem and work around, ensuring the tube isn't pinched.

Use tire levers to help fit the last section if necessary, but be careful not to pinch the tube.

7. Inflate the Tire

Use your pump or CO_2 inflator to inflate the tire to the recommended pressure.

8. Reinstall the Wheel

Place the wheel back onto the bike and secure the quick release or axle nuts.

Ensure the wheel is centered and the brake is re-engaged.

Liam's Trailside Flat Repair

Liam was midway through a challenging trail when he felt his rear tire go soft. Equipped with his repair kit, he quickly removed the wheel, patched the puncture, and reinstalled the tire. Thanks to his preparedness, he was back on the trail in no time.

Fixing a Broken Chain

Tools Needed

- Chain tool

- Quick link or spare chain pins

- Multi-tool (optional but often helpful)

Steps to Fix a Broken Chain

1. Remove the Broken Chain Link

Use the chain tool to push the pin out of the damaged link. Be careful not to push the pin all the way out; leave it in one plate to make reassembly easier.

2. Prepare the Quick Link (if applicable)

If using a quick link, remove another link to create open ends on the chain that the quick link can connect to.

3. Rejoin the Chain

Insert the quick link or new chain pin through the open ends.

If using a chain pin, use the chain tool to press the pin into place. Ensure it sits flush with the chain plates.

4. Check the Chain Movement

Flex the chain back and forth to ensure it moves freely. If it's stiff, gently work the chain to loosen it.

5. Reinstall the Chain

Re-thread the chain through the derailleur and around the chainring and cassette.

Shift through the gears to ensure the chain moves smoothly and correctly.

Emily's On-the-Go Chain Repair

During a weekend ride, Emily's chain snapped on a particularly rough section. She pulled out her multi-tool with a chain tool and quick link, removed the broken link, and rejoined the chain. With her quick fix, she completed her ride without further issues.

Final Thoughts

Being able to repair a flat tire or fix a broken chain on the trail is a vital skill for any mountain biker. It ensures you can handle common issues without needing assistance, allowing you to fully enjoy your ride. Regular practice of these repairs at home will make them second nature when you're out on the trail.

CHAPTER 8

Finding the Best Trails to Start With

What are some of the best beginner-friendly trails in my area?

Finding beginner-friendly trails is essential for new mountain bikers to build confidence and skills in a safe and enjoyable environment. Here's how you can discover some of the best beginner trails in your area:

Finding Fun Beginner Trails to Ride at the Start

Use Online Resources

Trailforks: This user-generated trail database is an excellent resource for finding trails of varying difficulty levels. Use the filters to find beginner trails.

Example: If you're in Colorado, search "Colorado beginner trails" on Trailforks. You might find options like the "Valmont Bike Park" in Boulder.

MTB Project: Similar to Trailforks, this app and website provide detailed trail information, user reviews, and difficulty ratings.

Example: In California, search for "California beginner trails" and find trails like "Big Bear Discovery Center Trail" in Big Bear Lake.

Pro Tip: We have both apps on our cell phones since we travel a lot and one will often have better information in an area than the other. Trailforks works best in Whistler Canada, for example.

Local Bike Shops

Ask for Recommendations: Staff at local bike shops often know the best trails for beginners. They can provide insider tips and maps.

Example: Visit your local shop and ask for beginner-friendly trails. They might direct you to a nearby park or a well-maintained trail system.

Join Local Biking Groups

Clubs and Online Forums: Many areas have mountain biking clubs or online forums where you can connect with other riders and get trail recommendations.

Example: Join a local Facebook group or look for biking clubs on Meet up.com. Members often organize rides suitable for beginners.

Check Out Municipal and State Parks

Parks and Recreation Departments: Many parks have designated mountain biking trails with various difficulty levels, including beginner-friendly options.

Example: Look at your city or state park's website. For example, Maryland's Patapsco Valley State Park offers excellent beginner trails like the "Glen Artney Area Trails."

Key Characteristics of Beginner-Friendly Trails

Wide and Smooth Paths: Trails with wide paths and smooth surfaces make it easier for beginners to navigate.

Gentle Elevation Changes: Look for trails with mild elevation changes and avoid steep climbs and descents.

Fewer Obstacles: Beginners should start on trails with minimal rocks, roots, and technical features.

Finding Trails in Oregon

Sarah, a new mountain biker in Portland, Oregon, wanted to find beginner-friendly trails. She checked Trailforks and discovered the "Sandy Ridge Trail System." Visiting her local bike shop confirmed this recommendation, as the staff mentioned the "Easy Climb" loop was perfect for beginners. Sarah also joined the "Portland Mountain Biking Club" on Facebook, where she found fellow beginners to ride with and share trail tips.

Final Thoughts

Beginner-friendly trails are the best way to start your mountain biking journey. Utilize online resources, local bike shops, and community groups to find the best options near you. Remember to look for trails that match your skill level, ensuring a fun and safe experience as you build your biking skills.

CHAPTER 9

Trails for Building your Skills

How can I find and choose trails that match my skill level?

Choosing trails that match your skill level is crucial for a safe and enjoyable mountain biking experience. Here's a guide to help you find and select the right trails:

Choosing the Best Trails for Your Perfect Ride

Understand Trail Difficulty Ratings

Green (Easy): Suitable for beginners. Wide paths, gentle gradients, and minimal obstacles.

Blue (Intermediate): For riders with some experience. More varied terrain with moderate gradients and some technical sections.

Black (Expert): For advanced riders. Steep, technical, and challenging trails with difficult obstacles.

Double Black (Pro): Very difficult, technical features, steep gradients, and not recommended for anyone but experts.

Use Trail Apps and Websites

Trailforks: Allows you to filter trails based on difficulty, user ratings, and location.

MTB Project: Offers detailed descriptions and user reviews that can help determine if a trail matches your skill level.

Example: Filtering for "blue trails" in Sedona, Arizona, can lead you to trails like "Bell Rock Pathway" that are great for intermediate riders.

Check Local Resources

Bike Shops: Staff recommendations are invaluable. They can suggest trails based on your skill level and provide additional tips.

Community Boards: Local forums, social media groups, and clubs often discuss trail conditions and difficulty.

Evaluate Trail Descriptions and Maps

Trail Descriptions: Pay attention to the descriptions for mentions of technical features, elevation changes, and overall difficulty.

Maps: Look at trail maps for elevation profiles and distances. Steep gradients and long distances may indicate higher difficulty.

Start with Easier Trails

Confidence Building: Begin with easier trails and gradually progress to more challenging ones as your skills improve.

Example: In North Carolina, start with the "Kerr Scott Trails" which offer various easy to intermediate options.

Consider Trail Conditions

Weather and Maintenance: Trails can become more difficult due to weather or lack of maintenance. Check recent trail reports for current conditions.

Example: A normally easy trail can become challenging if it's muddy or has been damaged by weather.

Get Feedback from Other Riders

Connect with Locals: Join group rides or ask fellow riders about their experiences with specific trails.

User Reviews: Look for detailed user reviews that mention specific challenges or highlights of a trail.

Finding Intermediate Trails in Utah

Jake, an intermediate rider in Utah, used Trailforks to find trails in the Moab area. By filtering for "blue trails," he found the "Bar M Loop," which matched his skill level. He confirmed this choice by visiting a local bike shop, where the staff recommended it as a fun and manageable trail for his level. Connecting with other riders in a local mountain biking group, Jake gathered additional tips and trail insights, ensuring a great riding experience.

Final Thoughts

Selecting the right trails for your skill level is vital for both safety and enjoyment. Use available tools, gather local insights, and constantly assess your progress to find the best trails that suit your abilities. Starting with easier trails and gradually working your way up will help you build confidence and skills efficiently.

CHAPTER 10

The Best Apps and Devices for Mountain Biking

What are the best resources for trail maps and navigation?

Having reliable resources for trail maps and navigation can greatly enhance your mountain biking experience. Here are some of the best tools and resources to help you navigate trails effectively:

Best Trail Apps

Because one will often have better trail information and reviews than the other in a given location, we have both on our phones.

Trailforks

Features: Extensive trail maps, user-generated content, difficulty ratings, and real-time trail conditions.

Availability: App available for iOS and Android, and a website with extensive trail information.

Example: In British Columbia, use Trailforks to find trails in the Whistler area, with detailed maps and trail reports.

MTB Project

Features: Detailed trail descriptions, user reviews, maps, photos, and elevation profiles.

Availability: App available for iOS and Android, and a comprehensive website.

Example: Navigate trails in Moab, Utah, with detailed maps and user reviews on MTB Project.

Best GPS Devices

Garmin Edge Series

Features: Turn-by-turn navigation, pre-loaded maps, and connectivity to trail apps like Trailforks and MTB Project.

Models: Garmin Edge 530 and 830 are popular choices for mountain bikers.

Example: Use Garmin Edge 530 to navigate through complex trail systems in areas like the Pisgah National Forest in North Carolina.

Wahoo ELEMNT Series

Features: Simple setup, turn-by-turn directions, and integration with various trail apps.

Models: Wahoo ELEMNT ROAM is an excellent device for navigation.

Example: Navigate the trail systems in the Bay Area, California, using Wahoo ELEMNT ROAM.

Best Paper Maps and Guidebooks

Local Maps

Available at visitor centers, bike shops, and state parks. They provide a reliable backup if technology fails.

Guidebooks

Books like "Mountain Bike America" series offer detailed maps and trail descriptions for specific regions.

Example: "Mountain Bike America: Arizona" provides comprehensive maps and trail guide for Arizona trails.

Best Online Trail Databases

AllTrails

Features: Comprehensive trail maps, user reviews, photos, and GPS tracking.

Availability: Website and app for iOS and Android.

Example: Find and navigate trails in the Pacific Northwest, with detailed guides and user-generated content.

OpenStreetMap (OSM)

Features: Open-source map that includes a wealth of trail information.

Availability: Available online and compatible with various GPS devices and apps.

Example: Useful for updating and navigating less-known trails.

Best Local Resources

Bike Shops

Local shops often provide maps and guidebooks, along with insider tips for navigating area trails.

Visitor Centers

Municipal, state, and national parks often have detailed maps and staff who can give advice.

Trail Organizations

Local mountain biking clubs and trail organizations frequently offer maps and navigation tips.

Example: The Trail Conservancy in places like Bentonville, Arkansas, offers maps and updates on trail conditions.

Pro Tip: Bentonville, Arkansas is an outstanding place to mountain bike. They have an extensive trail system that surrounds the town. They also have an extensive road bike path system. Basically, the town is built around cycling and if you like to ride you really should plan a trip to bike friendly Bentonville!

Navigating Trails in Vermont

Laura planned a mountain biking trip to Vermont. She started by using Trailforks to explore trails in the Stowe area. With her Garmin Edge 830, she downloaded the trails for offline use. At a local bike shop, she picked up a paper map as a backup and got recommendations from the staff. By combining these resources, Laura confidently navigated the trails and had a fantastic riding experience on trails she enjoyed without getting lost.

Final Thoughts

Effective navigation is critical for an enjoyable and safe mountain biking experience. Combining digital apps, GPS devices, and traditional paper maps ensures you are well-prepared for your ride. Regularly updating your navigation tools and seeking local insights will further enhance your trail navigation skills, making every ride a new adventure.

CHAPTER 11

Essential Protective Gear

What protective gear is essential for mountain biking?

Wearing the right protective gear when mountain biking is essential to prevent injuries and ensure a safe riding experience. Here's a comprehensive guide to the essential protective gear you should have:

Essential Gear for Every Ride

With the exception of the last two (optional) items, the following is gear that you should always have on you when you ride.

Helmet

Importance: A helmet is the most crucial piece of safety gear. It provides critical protection for your head in the event of a crash.

Types:

Half-Shell Helmets: Suitable for most types of mountain biking, providing protection for the top and back of the head.

Full-Face Helmets: Offer additional protection for the face and jaw, ideal for downhill and more aggressive riding.

Features: Look for features such as MIPS (Multi-directional Impact Protection System) for extra protection.

Example: The POC Tectal Race Spin helmet has advanced safety features and good ventilation.

Pro Tip: Make sure your helmet fits properly so that it does not slide around on your head when you are riding. This means it is snug but not too tight when placed on your head and it will stay on without the strap (for the most part) by simply turning/tightening the adjustment system at the back of the helmet. Our favorite helmet brands are Leatt, Fox, Bell and Giro. Definitely try before you buy because everyone's head is shaped differently!

Gloves

Importance: Gloves protect your hands from abrasions and blisters and improve grip on the handlebars. They will also prevent injury in a variety of emergency situations.

Types:

Full-Finger Gloves: Offer better protection and are suitable for various riding conditions.

Half-Finger Gloves: Provide more ventilation but less protection.

Example: Fox Ranger gel gloves offer excellent grip and protection for trail riding.

Eye Protection

Importance: Shields your eyes from wind, debris, branches, bugs, and harmful UV rays.

Sunglasses: Provide adequate protection for most riding conditions.

Goggles: Offer a more secure fit and better protection, especially for downhill riding.

Example: Oakley Radar EV Path sunglasses are popular for their quality and durability.

Pro Tip: we carry a pair of inexpensive clear safety glasses in our hydration packs in case our sunglasses break or it gets dark. There is nothing worse than tying to find your way home in the dark or after breaking your sunglasses when you can't see because the wind and/or rain is making your eyes tear.

Hydration Pack

Importance: Staying hydrated is crucial, and a hydration pack allows you to carry water and other essentials conveniently.

Features: Look for packs with a built-in water reservoir, multiple storage compartments, and comfortable straps.

Example: CamelBak Mule offers a 3L water reservoir and ample storage for a day on the trails.

Pro Tip: We always take our hydration packs, even for short rides when we don't think we will need water because they contain our bike repair kit and an emergency wind breaker. Both have come in handy on numerous occasions.

Protective Clothing

Importance: Specialized clothing can enhance comfort and protection. Because your bottom is in contact with a seat that is bouncing up and down, wearing padded bike shorts can be essential to having a good ride. This is even more important for women whose girl parts are easily chaffed leading to "saddle fatigue" long before the fun is over.

Types: Moisture-wicking jerseys, padded biking shorts, and waterproof jackets.

Example: Endura Hummvee waterproof jacket and padded shorts are popular choices for their comfort and durability.

Pro Tip: We always carry a lightweight wind breaker in our hydration pack. It is light, takes up minimal room and comes in handy when it gets colder later in the day or if fog rolls in. Just keeping the wind from penetrating your cloths makes a huge difference.

Knee and Elbow Pads (Optional but may be helpful at the start or when riding aggressively)

Importance: Protects joints from impacts and abrasions during falls.

Features: Look for flexible, comfortable, and breathable pads that do not restrict movement.

Example: G-Form Pro-X knee and elbow pads are lightweight and provide good protection without being bulky.

Body Armor (Optional but should be considered for aggressive riding or advanced trails)

Importance: Provides additional protection for the torso and back during aggressive or downhill riding.

Types: Can range from lightweight chest protectors to full body armor suits.

Example: Leatt Body Protector 3DF Airfit offers extensive protection with good airflow.

Pro Tip: Our son was a very aggressive rider and often went faster than his skills could handle. By insisting that he always wore body armor at the jump park, pump track or at mountain bike parks, he never ended having any serious injuries despite having lots of nasty crashes. Fortunately, he did grow out of it and today he is an avid mountain biker with excellent skills.

James's Safety Gear Setup

James, an avid mountain biker, always starts his ride with essential gear: a Bell Super 3R MIPS helmet, full-finger gloves, and G-Form knee pads. For eye protection, he uses Smith Squad MTB goggles. On longer rides, he carries a CamelBak Mule hydration pack to stay hydrated and store essentials like snacks, tools, and a first-aid kit. His gear has saved him from serious injuries on several occasions, allowing him to enjoy his rides with peace of mind.

Final Thoughts

Investing in the right protective gear is non-negotiable when it comes to mountain biking. Each piece of gear plays a crucial role in keeping you safe and comfortable on the trails. Ensure your gear fits well and meets safety standards to provide the best protection. Riding safely will help make the most out of your mountain biking adventures, allowing you to focus on the thrill of the ride.

CHAPTER 12

Riding Safely

How can I prevent injuries while riding?

Preventing injuries while riding is essential for enjoying mountain biking safely. Here are key strategies to help you stay injury-free on the trails:

Tips for Preventing Injuries

Wear Appropriate Protective Gear

Helmet: Always wear a properly fitted helmet and make sure chin strap is snug.

Padding: Use knee and elbow pads, gloves, and body armor as needed.

Ride Within Your Skill Level

Progress Gradually: Start with beginner trails and gradually progress to more challenging ones as your skills improve.

Avoid Overconfidence: Don't attempt trails or features beyond your ability. Practice and build your skills incrementally.

Know Your Trail

Scout New Trails: Walk or ride slowly through unfamiliar trails to get a sense of the terrain and obstacles.

Use Maps and Apps: Study trail maps and use apps like Trailforks or MTB Project to understand trail difficulty and conditions.

Maintain Your Bike

Regular Maintenance: Ensure your bike is in good working condition by performing regular checks and servicing.

Key Areas: Check tire pressure, brake function, chain condition, and suspension settings before every ride.

Use Proper Techniques

Body Position: Maintain a neutral or attack position for balance and control.

Braking: Use both brakes properly to avoid skidding and maintain control. Apply more pressure to the front brake while modulating the rear brake.

Weight Distribution: Shift your weight appropriately to maintain traction and stability on climbs, descents, and turns.

Stay Hydrated and Nourished

Hydration: Drink water regularly to stay hydrated, especially on long rides or hot days.

Nutrition: Carry snacks or energy bars to keep your energy levels stable.

Warm-Up and Stretching

Warm-Up: Engage in light cardio and dynamic stretches before riding to prepare your muscles.

Stretch Post-Ride: Stretch after riding to reduce muscle soreness and prevent injuries.

Ride with a Buddy

Safety in Numbers: Riding with a friend or group ensures help is available in case of an accident.

Emergency Plans: Know each other's emergency contact information and have a plan in place.

First-Aid Knowledge

Carry a Kit: Always carry a small first-aid kit with essentials like bandages, antiseptic wipes, and pain relievers.

Basic Skills: Learn basic first-aid skills to handle minor injuries on the trail.

Sarah's Injury Prevention Routine

Sarah, an experienced rider, always warms up with dynamic stretches and light cardio before hitting the trails. She wears a full set of protective gear, including a helmet, gloves, and knee pads. Sarah regularly inspects her bike and uses apps like Trailforks to scout new trails. Riding with a group, she ensures there's always someone to assist in case of an accident. These practices have helped her prevent serious injuries and enjoy her rides safely.

Final Thoughts

Preventing injuries while mountain biking involves a combination of wearing the right gear, knowing your limits, maintaining your bike, and using proper techniques. Staying hydrated, warming up, and riding with a buddy further enhance your safety. By adopting these strategies, you can minimize the risk of injuries and focus on the exhilarating experience of mountain biking.

CHAPTER 13

Gear Checklist

What should I pack for a day of mountain biking?

Packing the right items for a day of mountain biking ensures you're prepared for various situations you may encounter on the trail. Here's a comprehensive guide to what you should pack:

What to Bring When You Ride

Essential Gear:

Helmet

Always wear a properly fitted helmet to protect your head.

Protective Padding

Knee and elbow pads, gloves, and eye protection (sunglasses or goggles).

Hydration Pack or Water Bottle

Ensure you have sufficient water, especially for longer rides. A hydration pack with a reservoir is ideal.

Weather-Appropriate Clothing

Wear moisture-wicking jersey and padded cycling shorts for comfort.

Pack a lightweight waterproof jacket in case of rain.

Tools and Repair Kit

Multi-Tool

A multi-tool with various Allen wrenches, screwdrivers, and a chain tool.

Pump or CO2 Inflator

To inflate tires if you get a flat.

Spare Tube and Patch Kit

Essential for fixing flat tires.

Tire Levers

For removing tires during repairs.

Chain Links or Quick Link

For repairing a broken chain.

Spare Derailleur Hanger

In case the existing hanger gets bent or broken.

Duct Tape and Zip Ties

Versatile tools for temporary fixes.

First-Aid Kit

Small First-Aid Kit

Include bandages, antiseptic wipes, pain relievers, and any personal medications.

Food and Nutrition

Energy Bars/Gels

Easy-to-carry snacks to keep your energy levels stable.

Protein, Healthy Fats, Fruit or Nuts

Healthy snacks to sustain you through the ride. We like beef jerky, free-range beef hot dogs, Kind bars and apples with peanut butter.

Navigation and Communication

Trail Map or App

Carry a physical map of the trail or use a navigation app like Trailforks or MTB Project.

GPS Device or Bike Computer

For accurate navigation.

Mobile Phone

Fully charged phone for emergencies.

Portable Charger

To keep your devices powered up.

Safety and Convenience

ID and Emergency Contact Information

Carry personal identification and contact details.

Cash and Cards

For emergencies or unexpected needs.

Insect Repellent and Sunscreen

Protect yourself from bugs and UV rays.

Whistle or Small Alarm

In case you need to signal for help.

Alex's Day Ride Checklist

Alex, a seasoned rider, follows a comprehensive checklist before his day rides. He packs his CamelBak Mule with water, a multi-tool, a spare tube, tire levers, and a portable pump. In addition to some beef jerky, a Kind bar and a first-aid kit, he includes a trail map, his smartphone with navigation apps, and a lightweight waterproof jacket. Alex's well-prepared approach has aided him on numerous occasions, from repairing flat tires to navigating unexpected weather changes.

Final Thoughts

Packing appropriately for a day of mountain biking ensures you're prepared for various scenarios, making your ride safer and more enjoyable. By including essential gear, tools, first-aid supplies, nutrition, navigation tools, and safety items, you'll be ready to handle most challenges on the trail. Preparation enhances your ride, allowing you to focus on the adventure and thrill of mountain biking.

CHAPTER 14

Fitness and Training

What exercises can I do to improve my strength and endurance for mountain biking?

Improving your strength and endurance is crucial for enhancing your mountain biking performance and enjoying longer rides. Here are some exercises specifically designed to target the muscles and energy systems you use while mountain biking:

Cardiovascular Exercises

Cycling Intervals

Why: Builds cardiovascular endurance and mimics the varied intensity of mountain biking.

How to Perform: Perform intervals on a stationary bike or road bike. Warm up for 10 minutes, then alternate between high-intensity pedaling (1-2 minutes) and low-intensity recovery (2-4 minutes). Repeat for 20-30 minutes.

Running

Why: Improves cardiovascular fitness and leg strength.

How to Perform: Incorporate steady-state runs and interval training into your routine. Aim for 30-60 minutes of running, 3-4 times a week.

Rowing

Why: Provides a full-body workout that enhances cardiovascular endurance and upper body strength.

How to Perform: Use a rowing machine for 20-30 minutes, focusing on maintaining a steady pace.

Strength Training

Squats

Why: Strengthens the legs, glutes, and core, crucial for powerful pedaling and stability.

How to Perform: Stand with feet shoulder-width apart, bend your knees and lower into a squat position, keeping your back straight and chest up. Return to standing. Perform 3 sets of 12-15 reps.

Example: Regular squats, goblet squats with a dumbbell, and barbell back squats.

Lunges

Why: Builds unilateral leg strength and balance.

How to Perform: Step forward with one leg and lower your hips until both knees are bent at a 90-degree angle. Push back to the starting position. Alternate legs. Perform 3 sets of 10 reps per leg.

Deadlifts

Why: Strengthens the posterior chain, including the hamstrings, glutes, and lower back.

How to Perform: Stand with feet hip-width apart, hold a barbell or dumbbells in front of you, bend at the hips and knees while keeping your back straight, and lift the weight by standing up. Perform 3 sets of 10-12 reps.

Planks

Why: Enhances core stability, which is essential for maintaining control and balance on the bike.

How to Perform: Hold a plank position—shoulders over elbows, body in a straight line—for 30-60 seconds. Perform 3 sets.

Push-Ups

Why: Strengthens the chest, shoulders, and triceps, improving upper body endurance and control.

How to Perform: Perform a traditional push-up with hands shoulder-width apart and body in a straight line. Lower your chest to the floor and push back up. Perform 3 sets of 12-15 reps.

Flexibility and Mobility

Dynamic Stretching

Why: Improves flexibility and prepares your muscles for riding.

How to Perform: Incorporate dynamic stretches like leg swings, arm circles, and hip openers into your warm-up routine.

Yoga

Why: Enhances flexibility, balance, and mental focus.

How to Perform: Attend a yoga class or follow online sessions that focus on poses beneficial for cyclists, such as downward dog, pigeon pose, and child's pose.

Pro Tip: Yoga is a great way to reverse the strain your body goes thru maintaining your riding position. Sandy, in particular, appreciates the chest opening exercises and twists as they help release strain and relieve pain in her back which can get overworked on really tough, long rides. In addition, the flexibility she gains makes it far more likely she will not do any permanent injury when she falls.

Mark's Training Regimen

Mark, a dedicated mountain biker, incorporates a structured training regimen into his weekly routine. He starts with cycling intervals on weekdays to improve his cardiovascular endurance. Strength training is a key component, with sessions including squats, lunges, and planks. Every weekend, Mark goes for a long run to boost his stamina further. Yoga sessions twice a week enhance his flexibility and aid recovery. This balanced approach significantly improves his performance on challenging trails.

Final Thoughts

Combining cardiovascular exercises, strength training, and flexibility work is the key to enhancing your strength and endurance for mountain biking. By targeting the specific muscles and energy systems used in the sport, you'll ride longer, stronger, and more efficiently. Consistent training not only improves performance but also reduces the risk of injury, making each ride more enjoyable.

CHAPTER 15

Creating a Training Plan

Question 15: How can I create a training plan that fits my schedule?

Creating a personalized training plan that fits your schedule is essential for consistent progress and avoiding burnout. Here's a step-by-step guide to developing a manageable and effective training plan:

Assess Your Goals and Schedule

Identify Your Goals

Determine what you want to achieve: Whether it's improving endurance, increasing strength, or preparing for a race.

Evaluate Your Schedule

Analyze your weekly schedule to identify available time slots for training. Consider work hours, family commitments, and other responsibilities.

Structure Your Training Plan

Weekly Training Schedule

Cardio Workouts: Include 3-4 sessions per week. Mix high-intensity intervals, steady-state rides, and cross-training activities like running or rowing.

Strength Training: Aim for 2-3 sessions per week, focusing on compound movements like squats, deadlifts, and planks.

Flexibility and Mobility: Incorporate yoga or dynamic stretching 2-3 times a week, preferably on rest or light workout days.

Rest Days: Schedule 1-2 rest days per week to allow for recovery and prevent overtraining.

Example Weekly Plan

- Monday: Cardio intervals (30-45 minutes)

- Tuesday: Strength training (45-60 minutes)

- Wednesday: Steady-state cardio (45-60 minutes)

- Thursday: Yoga or dynamic stretching (30-45 minutes)

- Friday: Strength training (45-60 minutes)

- Saturday: Long ride or run (60-120 minutes)

- Sunday: Rest or active recovery (light stretching or walk)

Balance Intensity and Volume

Vary Intensity: Alternate between high-intensity workouts and moderate-intensity sessions to avoid burnout and overtraining.

Progress Gradually: Increase the duration and intensity of your workouts gradually to build endurance and strength steadily.

Listen to Your Body

Adapt to Changes: Be flexible with your training plan. If you feel fatigued or sore, adjust your workouts accordingly.

Monitor Recovery: Ensure you're getting enough sleep, nutrition, and hydration to support recovery and performance.

Track Your Progress

Use a Training Log

Keep a training log to track your workouts, progress, and any adjustments. This helps in identifying patterns and making informed changes.

Set Milestones

Set short-term milestones to keep you motivated and focused on your long-term goals.

Sophie's Balanced Training Plan

Sophie, a busy professional and mountain biking enthusiast, designed a training plan that fits her hectic schedule. With weekday work commitments, she schedules cardio intervals on Mondays and strength training on Tuesdays and Fridays. Wednesday is her day for a steady-state run, while Thursday is reserved for a yoga session to improve flexibility. Saturdays are dedicated to long rides, exploring local trails, and Sundays are rest days. Sophie tracks her progress using a training log, making adjustments as needed, ensuring a balanced approach that accommodates her work-life balance.

Final Thoughts

Creating a training plan tailored to your goals and schedule is crucial for consistent improvement and injury prevention. By balancing cardio, strength, and flexibility workouts and allowing for adequate rest, you can progress effectively without feeling overwhelmed.

Listen to your body, adjust your plan as needed, and track your progress for the best results. A well-structured plan will help you stay motivated and enjoy every ride, making your mountain biking journey fulfilling and rewarding.

CHAPTER 16

Fueling Your Body

What nutrition tips should I follow to fuel my mountain biking adventures?

Proper nutrition is crucial for fueling your mountain biking adventures and ensuring peak performance. If you ride with kids, in particular, you will want to be sure to bring appropriate snacks since nothing ruins a great ride more than gnawing hunger. Perhaps more important that what TO is is what NOT TO eat.

General Nutrition Principals

Eliminate Processed Foods

Everyone's health generally improves by cutting out packaged and processed foods. Unless they clearly state otherwise and prove it with a recognizable ingredient list, most packaged food manufacturers aim to make food irresistible (read: addictive). They often use chemicals that your body isn't familiar with and offer no proven nutritional value (you're basically a test subject).

Reduce "White Stuff"

Many athletes benefit from eliminating white, sugary, or starchy foods that break down quickly and spike blood glucose. This includes not only table sugar, but also white potatoes, white rice, white bread, corn chips, and similar items. Yes, I feel your pain! But cutting out simple carbohydrates can make a huge difference. This is especially true if you often feel your energy crash during workouts or in the afternoon, need lots of coffee to wake up, or feel ravenous shortly after breakfast.

My Personal Experience with Nutrition

I completed the **Death Ride Tour of the California Alps** twice. The Death Ride is over 100 miles with more than 14,000 feet of climbing over three high-altitude mountain passes. The first year, I ate a high-carb spaghetti dinner the night before and enjoyed all the sugary, high-carb snacks and energy drinks offered along the ride. I almost didn't make it! I hit the wall hard, and although I finished, it was one of the most painful things I've ever done.

I had no plans to ride the Death Ride again, but then I changed my diet by eliminating gluten, sugar, simple carbs, and packaged foods. Suddenly, I had much more energy, and my workouts felt energizing again. I felt so much better that I signed up for the ride again. This time, I had a high-protein dinner the night before and limited my snacks during the race to nuts, beef jerky, and bananas with peanut butter. I drank only water mixed with plain electrolyte packets. The results were incredible. Not only did I finish 30 minutes faster the second time, but I also felt good during the entire ride—tired, but good!

The following year, I got married and had kids, so I never rode the Death Ride again. If I hadn't been busy with family life, I would have liked to try it on a Ketogenic or Carnivore diet. Many successful pro-athletes and ultra-distance runners have switched to running on ketones, staying in a permanent state of "runner's high." They report more energy and better muscle recovery. Their bodies essentially function as a competitor's body does after hitting the wall and switching to running on fat (ketones). Since their bodies are already adapted to it, they avoid the significant pain that usually comes with this switch.

Although I now cycle between eating a paleo, keto and carnivore diet, I'll never experience the Death Ride difference personally. I sold my road-race bike after having kids. I always preferred training on the dirt over the pavement anyway. Bottom line—I don't like worrying about the kids getting hit by a car, and we all love being out in the woods on trails, hitting the occasional (in my case) or every big jump (in the kids' case).

Pre-Ride Nutrition

Carbohydrates

Importance: Provides a readily available source of energy.

What to Eat: Include complex carbohydrates such as oatmeal, whole grain bread, fruits, and vegetables.

Timing: Eat a balanced meal with carbs 2-3 hours before your ride.

Proteins

Importance: Supports muscle repair and growth.

What to Eat: Incorporate lean proteins like chicken, fish, yogurt, and eggs in your pre-ride meal.

Hydration

Importance: Prevents dehydration and maintains performance.

What to Drink: Drink 16-20 ounces of water 2-3 hours before your ride, and another 8 ounces 30 minutes before starting.

During the Ride

Hydration

Guidelines: Drink small amounts of water regularly to stay hydrated.

What to Bring: A hydration pack or water bottles. For longer rides, consider electrolyte drinks.

Carbohydrates

Quick Energy: Consume easily digestible carbs to maintain energy levels.

What to Eat: Energy gels, chews, bananas, and dried fruits.

Frequency: Aim for 30-60 grams of carbs per hour, depending on the ride intensity and duration.

Post-Ride Nutrition

What you eat after your ride is important because it can either speed up or slow down your recovery.

Protein

Importance: Aids in muscle recovery and repair. Protein is the single most important thing for you to consume after riding

What to Eat: Include protein-rich foods like red meat (preferred), fish, chicken, shell fish, a protein shake, dairy, or plant-based protein sources.

Timing: Consume within 30 minutes to 2 hours after your ride.

Rehydration

Importance: Restores fluid balance and helps to prevent leg cramps.

What to Drink: Water with added electrolytes, or recovery drinks designed for athletes.

Pro Tip: For rapid recovery and to support a healthy lifestyle, avoid workout drinks that are packed with sugar and corn syrup. A much better choice is pure spring water with an added electrolyte package like LMNT Electrolytes.

Carbohydrates

Importance: Replenishes glycogen stores.

What to Eat: A mix of simple and complex carbs like sweet potatoes, rice, fruits, and whole grain pasta.

Pro Tip: Samantha follows a carnivore diet (no carbohydrates), meaning that her body runs off of ketones instead of glycogen stores. When she switched her diet she was surprised to discover that she no longer gets sore after workouts and she no longer runs out of energy on long rides.

General Nutrition Tips

Balanced Diet

Importance: Supports overall health and performance.

Components: A diet rich in fruits, vegetables, lean proteins, healthy fats, and whole grains.

Snack Smart

On-the-Go: Carry healthy snacks like beef jerky, nuts, seeds, yogurt, and fruit for sustained energy. Avoid sugary snacks as they will spike your blood sugar causing a crash afterwards leaving you irritable and hungry.

Listen to Your Body:

Cravings and Needs: Pay attention to your body's signals and adjust your nutrition accordingly.

> Here are two very different nutritional approaches followed by serious competitors, both of which enable them to be winners in national competitions. Different strokes for different folks! Your job is to discover what works best for you.
>
> ## Nutritional Strategy on Race Day: Two very different yet successful approaches
>
> Jacob, a competitive mountain biker, follows a strict nutrition plan to optimize his performance. Before a race, he consumes a breakfast of oatmeal with fruits and a protein shake 2-3 hours ahead. During the race, he relies on energy gels every 45 minutes and hydration packs with electrolyte drinks. After the race, Jacob refuels with a balanced meal of grilled chicken, quinoa, and vegetables, accompanied by a protein shake. His meticulous approach helps sustain energy levels and aids in rapid recovery.
>
> Anthony, also a competitive mountain biker follows a carnivore diet to optimize his performance. He will often fast before a race, preferring that 100% of his energy goes towards his performance, not digestion. Since his body runs off of Ketones instead of carbohydrates, he has a consistent source of energy without the need to eat. During the race he will only consume spring water with plain electrolytes. After the race he enjoys ribeye steak, prime rib, bacon and eggs until he is completely satiated. The next day his muscles are usually 100% recovered and he will have a light workout just to keep his blood moving.

Final Thoughts

Effective nutrition is fundamental to performing well and recovering quickly in mountain biking. By focusing on pre-ride fuel, maintaining energy and hydration during the ride, and nourishing your body post-ride, you can maximize your performance and enjoyment on the trails. A balanced diet, mindful snacking, and listening to your body's needs will support your overall fitness and enhance your mountain biking adventures.

CHAPTER 17

Finding People to Ride With

How can I find people to ride with and connect with local mountain biking groups or clubs?

Connecting with local mountain biking groups and clubs is a great way to find riding partners, learn new skills, and become a part of the mountain biking community. Here's how you can find and connect with these groups:

Online Platforms

Meetup

How to Use: Visit Meetup.com and search for mountain biking groups in your area. Join the groups that interest you.

Example: In Colorado, you might find groups like "Denver Mountain Biking Meetup" which organize regular group rides and events.

Facebook Groups

How to Use: Use Facebook's search function to find local mountain biking groups. Join the groups and participate in discussions.

Example: Search for groups like "Mountain Bikers of Seattle" to connect with other riders in the Seattle area.

Reddit

How to Use: Join subreddits dedicated to mountain biking, such as r/MTB or r/mountainbiking. Look for local threads or create a post asking for group recommendations in your area.

Example: Post on r/mountainbiking asking for group rides in the Boston area.

Local Bike Shops

Ask for Recommendations

How to Use: Visit local bike shops and ask the staff about local clubs or group rides. They often have information about community events and rides.

Example: Walk into a shop like "Revolution Cycles" in Washington, D.C., and inquire about weekly group rides.

Bulletin Boards

How to Use: Many bike shops have bulletin boards or flyers advertising local rides and events. Check these regularly for updates.

Bike Parks and Trails

Join Events

How to Use: Participate in events organized at local bike parks and trails, which are great opportunities to meet other riders.

Example: Attend events at places like "Whistler Bike Park" in British Columbia, where you can join group rides and meet new biking friends.

Talk to Fellow Riders

How to Use: Approach riders you meet on the trails. Introduce yourself and ask if they're part of any clubs or know of local group rides.

Mountain Biking Organizations

IMBA (International Mountain Bicycling Association)

How to Use: Visit the IMBA website to find local chapters near you. Join a chapter to get involved in group rides and trail building activities.

Example: Find a local chapter like "Mid-Atlantic Off-Road Enthusiasts (MORE)" if you live in the D.C. area.

Local Clubs and Associations

How to Use: Research regional clubs or associations that organize rides and events.

Example: Join the "San Diego Mountain Biking Association (SDMBA)" to connect with riders in Southern California.

Pro Tip: Many of the local clubs organize community events, have booths in local festivals and sponsor trail work days. Some of the very best trails we have ridden we learned about thru our local organization because they were instrumental in having the trails built via a partnership with our county parks system. In addition, it is nice to spend time with people you enjoy riding with in other social situations. You local clubs can often use your support to maintain the local trails and to work with the local community to expand trail systems.

Group Rides and Clinics

Join Group Rides

How to Use: Many clubs and bike shops organize regular group rides. Sign up for these to meet other riders.

Example: Look for local rides posted by your area's chapter on Trailforks or MTB Project.

Attend Skills Clinics

How to Use: Sign up for mountain biking skills clinics, often advertised by bike shops or clubs.

Example: Attend workshops organized by "Ladies AllRide" to improve your skills and meet other women riders.

Connecting in Austin, Texas

Jane, new to Austin, wanted to find mountain biking buddies. She joined the "Austin Mountain Bikers Meetup" group on Meetup.com and participated in a few rides. She also visited "Mellow Johnny's Bike Shop," where staff advised her about weekly rides and local trails. By attending these group rides, Jane quickly connected with other mountain biking enthusiasts, creating new friendships and getting insider tips on the best trails in the area.

Final Thoughts

Connecting with local mountain biking groups or clubs enhances your riding experience, offering camaraderie, support, and opportunities to learn and grow as a rider. Utilize online platforms, local bike shops, and community events to find and engage with fellow mountain bikers. Being part of a community not only enriches your journey but also makes every ride more enjoyable and memorable.

CHAPTER 18

Participating in Events and Races

What are some popular mountain biking events or races I can participate in?

Participating in mountain biking events and races is a fantastic way to challenge yourself, meet other riders, and immerse yourself in the biking community. Here are some popular events and races you might consider:

Endurance Races

Leadville Trail 100 MTB (Colorado)

Description: Known as one of the toughest mountain bike races, this 100-mile race tests endurance and grit at high elevations.

Example: Riders from around the world come to Leadville, Colorado, to test their limits in this iconic race.

Dirty Kanza (Kansas)

Description: This 200-mile gravel race, now part of the Lifetime Grand Prix, is known for its challenging course and intense competition.

Example: Cyclists navigate through the Flint Hills of Kansas, often contending with unpredictable weather and rough terrain.

Cross-Country (XC) Races

Sea Otter Classic (California)

Description: A premier cycling festival that includes cross-country races, downhill competitions, and a massive expo.

Example: Held in Monterey, California, the Sea Otter Classic attracts riders of all levels, offering a variety of races and events.

Whiskey Off-Road (Arizona)

Description: A challenging and scenic XC race in Prescott, Arizona, featuring various distance options from 15 to 50 miles.

Example: Riders tackle technical singletrack and demanding climbs, enjoying the natural beauty of the Prescott National Forest.

Downhill (DH) Races

Crankworx Festival (Multiple Locations)

Description: An international mountain biking festival featuring downhill, slopestyle, and other gravity events.

Example: Held in Whistler, British Columbia, Crankworx attracts top riders and spectators from around the world.

Red Bull Hardline (Wales)

Description: One of the most extreme downhill races, known for its treacherous course and massive jumps.

Example: Held in the Welsh countryside, this event pushes even the most skilled riders to their limits.

Multi-Day Stage Races

BC Bike Race (British Columbia)

Description: A seven-day stage race through British Columbia's breathtaking trails, known for its challenging terrain and scenic views.

Example: Riders experience everything from lush forests to rugged mountains, making it a bucket-list event for many.

Cape Epic (South Africa)

Description: An eight-day stage race in South Africa, considered one of the toughest mountain bike races globally.

Example: Teams of two navigate through diverse landscapes, facing heat, dust, and technical trails.

Gravel and Adventure Races

Belgian Waffle Ride (California)

Description: A unique race featuring a mix of road, gravel, and dirt, challenging riders with its varied terrain.

Example: Held in San Diego, this race tests riders' versatility and endurance over a grueling course.

Grinduro (Various Locations)

Description: Combines gravel racing with enduro-style timed segments, offering a mix of competition and camaraderie.

Example: Events are held in picturesque locations worldwide, from California to Scotland.

Women-Specific Events

Grit Clinics (Various Locations)

Description: Skills clinics designed specifically for women, offering instruction and community building.

Example: Held in various locations across the U.S., these clinics provide a supportive environment for women to improve their riding skills.

Revolution Enduro (Colorado)

Description: A women's enduro racing series in Colorado, focused on creating a positive and inclusive racing atmosphere.

Example: Riders compete in multiple downhill stages, fostering both competition and community.

Entering the Sea Otter Classic

Emma, an intermediate rider, decided to participate in the Sea Otter Classic. She registered for the XC race and trained rigorously, improving her endurance and technical skills. The event offered her a chance to ride alongside professionals and amateurs alike, enjoy the festival atmosphere, and attend the expo to check out the latest gear. The experience was both challenging and exhilarating, and she left with new friendships, memories, and a sense of accomplishment.

Final Thoughts

Participating in mountain biking events and races offers unique opportunities to challenge yourself, meet fellow riders, and immerse yourself in the biking culture. Whether you're interested in endurance races, cross-country competitions, downhill thrills, or multi-day adventures, there's an event out there for you. Signing up for events not only pushes your limits but also connects you with the vibrant mountain biking community, making every ride an unforgettable experience.

CHAPTER 19

Supporting the Sport of Mountain Biking

How can I contribute to and support trail maintenance and advocacy efforts?

Supporting trail maintenance and advocacy efforts is crucial for preserving and enhancing mountain biking trails. Here's how you can contribute to these efforts:

Join a Local Trail Association

Find Local Organizations

Research local trail or mountain biking associations and become a member.

Example: Join the "Mid-Atlantic Off-Road Enthusiasts (MORE)" if you live in the Mid-Atlantic region.

Participate in Trail Work Days

Attend organized trail work days to help maintain and build trails.

Example: Volunteer for trail maintenance events organized by your local IMBA chapter or biking club.

Donate

Financial Contributions

Donate to trail associations or non-profits dedicated to trail maintenance and advocacy.

Example: Contribute to organizations like the "Trail Trust" or "Local Motion" that focus on outdoor recreation and trail upkeep.

In-Kind Donations

Provide tools, equipment, or supplies needed for trail work.

Example: Donate shovels, rakes, or other tools to your local chapter performing trail maintenance work.

Advocate for Trails

Attend Public Meetings

Participate in public meetings or hearings regarding trail access and land use.

Example: Attend city council meetings or park board hearings to advocate for maintaining or expanding trail networks.

Engage with Local Politicians

Write to or meet with local representatives to express the importance of trails and green space.

Example: Connect with politicians in your area to discuss policies that support trail development and preservation.

Lead or Join Advocacy Groups

Form or Join a Committee

We Need You! Get involved with trail committees or advocacy groups within your community or biking club.

Example: Join advocacy groups like "People for Bikes" or "Rails-to-Trails Conservancy" to take part in broader initiatives.

Educate and Promote

Raise Awareness

Use social media, blogs, or newsletters to educate others about the importance of trail maintenance.

Example: Share trail condition updates, maintenance events, and success stories on platforms like Instagram or community forums.

Host Events

Organize events like trail awareness rides, clean-up days, or fundraising events.

Example: Host a "Trail Appreciation Day" where local riders gather to work on trails and celebrate their efforts with a group ride.

Practice Responsible Riding

Follow Trail Etiquette

Respect trail rules and guidelines, minimize your impact, and encourage others to do the same.

Example: Yield to other trail users, stay on designated trails, and avoid riding in wet or muddy conditions to prevent trail damage.

Report Issues

Notify local trail organizations of any issues like fallen trees, erosion, or vandalism.

Example: Use apps like Trailforks to report trail conditions directly to the organization managing the trails.

Supporting Trail Maintenance in Vermont

Tom, an avid mountain biker in Vermont, is a member of the "Vermont Mountain Bike Association (VMBA)." He regularly participates in trail workdays, helping to maintain the popular Kingdom Trails. Additionally, Tom donates to VMBA and engages with local government representatives to advocate for sustainable trail development. His efforts, along with those of the community, ensure that the trails remain in excellent condition for all users to enjoy.

Final Thoughts

Contributing to and supporting trail maintenance and advocacy efforts is essential for sustaining and improving the mountain biking experience. By joining local trail associations, donating, advocating, and educating others, you can make a meaningful impact. Practicing responsible riding and participating in community events further enhances trail sustainability. Your involvement ensures that trails remain accessible and enjoyable for future generations of mountain bikers.

Section Two
Evolving Your Riding Experience

Evolving Your Riding Experience

Now that we got you started on the right foot, lets cover some fun and important topics now that you have the basics and should not be feeling overwhelmed. Remember, KEEP IT FUN!!

Here Is What We Cover In Section Two

Intermediate Skill Development and Riding Techniques

- Tips for evolving your skills and mastering riding techniques that offer greater control so you can tackle increasingly challenging terrain.

Advanced Skills and Riding Techniques

- Tips for mastering advanced skills for tackling extreme terrains, performing jumps, navigating switchbacks, and handling rock gardens with confidence.

Seasonal Riding Tips

- Advice on riding in different seasons like winter and summer when the temperatures may be very hot or the ground may be muddy.

Youth and Family Biking

- Tips for engaging young riders and enjoying family-friendly biking experiences.

First Aid and Safety

- Basic first aid techniques and safety tips for dealing with common injuries on the trail.

Traveling with Your Bike

- Tips for transporting your bike safely and legally, both domestically and internationally.

Biking Adventures

- Guide for preparing for multi-day trips, essential packing tips, and managing difficult terrain.

Bike Technology and Innovations

- Latest trends in mountain biking technology, including new materials, bike geometries, and smart accessories.

CHAPTER 20

Intermediate Skill Development and Riding Techniques

What skills should I focus on developing and what riding techniques can I learn to tackle more challenging trails?

Taking on more challenging trails requires mastering riding techniques that offer greater control, stability, and confidence. Here's an in-depth guide to some essential skills you will want to focus on as you gain time and experience in the saddle:

Cornering

Bermed Corners

How to Perform: Approach the bermed corner with moderate speed. Lean your bike into the turn while keeping your body more upright. Look ahead through the turn to where you want to go. Use your outside foot to apply pressure, keeping it down.

Tip: Flow through the berm by committing to the lean and maintaining a steady speed.

Flat Corners

How to Perform: Enter the corner wide and brake before the turn. Lean your bike beneath you while keeping your body more upright. Feather the brakes if needed to maintain traction.

Tip: Keep your weight centered and avoid sudden movements that could lose traction.

Technical Descents

Steep Drops

How to Perform: Approach slowly and shift your weight back as you descend. Keep your arms and knees bent to absorb impact and maintain control. Feather the brakes to control your speed.

Tip: Look ahead to where you want to go, not just at the immediate drop.

Rock Gardens

How to Perform: Approach with moderate speed. Use a light touch on the handlebars and let the bike move beneath you. Keep your pedals level and use your legs and arms as suspension.

Tip: Keep a steady line, and avoid braking or sudden steering corrections.

Jumps and Drops

Small Jumps

How to Perform: Approach with moderate speed. As your front wheel leaves the ground, pull up on the handlebars and push down with your legs to lift the rear wheel. Stay centered over the bike.

Tip: Practice on smaller jumps before progressing to larger ones.

Drops

How to Perform: Shift your weight back and extend your arms and legs as you go off the drop. Look ahead and stay relaxed.

Tip: Start with small drops and gradually increase the height as you gain confidence.

Manuals and Wheelies

Manuals

How to Perform: Shift your weight back and pull up on the handlebars without pedaling. Your arms should remain extended while your body leans back. Balance by shifting your weight.

Tip: Practice on flat ground before attempting manuals on trails.

Wheelies

How to Perform: Pedal hard while pulling up on the handlebars. Keep your weight centered and use your rear brake to control the balance point.

Tip: Start with one pedal stroke and gradually increase the duration as you improve your balance.

Climbing Technical Sections

Rocky Climbs

How to Perform: Shift to a low gear before the climb. Stay seated to maintain traction on the rear wheel. Lean slightly forward to keep the front wheel down.

Tip: Keep a steady cadence and choose a smooth line.

Loose Terrain

How to Perform: Maintain a steady and controlled speed. Stay seated and use a light touch on the handlebars to avoid slipping.

Tip: Avoid sudden changes in speed or direction that could cause loss of traction.

Mastering Technical Descents

Jake, an intermediate rider, wanted to improve his skills on technical descents. He practiced on smaller features before tackling larger rock gardens. By focusing on technique—keeping his weight back, using his arms and legs as suspension, and maintaining a steady speed—Jake gained confidence and control. He also took a skills clinic focused on technical riding, further refining his abilities. Now, he navigates challenging descents with ease and enjoys the thrill of mastering difficult trails.

Final Thoughts

Learning advanced riding techniques enables you to tackle more challenging trails with confidence and control. Practice these skills regularly, starting with smaller features and gradually progressing to more difficult ones. Taking skills clinics or lessons can also accelerate your learning. Mastery of these techniques not only enhances your riding experience but also opens up new and exciting trails to explore.

CHAPTER 21

Advanced Skills and Techniques

How can I develop skills for handling extreme terrains, performing jumps, mastering switchbacks, and navigating rock gardens?

Mastering advanced mountain biking skills is essential for tackling extreme terrains, performing jumps, navigating switchbacks, and handling rock gardens with confidence. Here's a detailed guide to help you enhance your abilities and ride more challenging trails effectively.

Handling Extreme Terrains

Understanding Terrain Types

Rocky Terrain: Characterized by loose rocks, boulders, and uneven ground.

Rooty Terrain: Filled with exposed tree roots, often found in forested areas.

Loose and Steep Climbs: Unstable surfaces combined with steep inclines.

Techniques for Rocky Terrain

Body Position: Maintain an attack position—stand on your pedals with knees and elbows bent, and your weight centered over the bike.

Line Choice: Choose the smoothest line, avoiding larger rocks when possible. Look ahead to plan your path.

Momentum: Keep a steady, controlled speed to avoid getting stuck between rocks. Use your body as suspension.

Example: On a rocky descent in Moab, John kept a loose grip on the handlebars, allowing the bike to navigate over the rocks while maintaining balance in the attack position.

Techniques for Rooty Terrain

Body Position: Similar to rocky terrain, keep an attack position to adapt quickly to sudden root encounters.

Pedal Timing: Time your pedal strokes to avoid hitting roots. Maintain level pedals when approaching sections filled with roots.

Momentum: Ensure you have enough speed to roll over the roots without getting caught.

Example: Lisa practiced timing her pedal strokes and shifted her weight back slightly when rolling over large roots on a forest trail.

Techniques for Loose and Steep Climbs

Seated Climbing: Stay seated to maintain traction on the rear wheel. Lean slightly forward to keep the front wheel down.

Gear Management: Shift to a low gear before the climb and maintain a steady cadence.

Smooth Power Application: Apply power smoothly to avoid wheel spin.

Example: Sarah used a low gear and kept her weight balanced over the bike on a loose, steep climb, allowing her to maintain traction and climb efficiently.

Performing Jumps

Types of Jumps

Tabletops: Jumps with a flat top, ideal for beginners.

Gap Jumps: Jumps with a gap between the takeoff and landing points, requiring more skill.

Step-Ups: Jumps where the landing is higher than the takeoff, requiring precise timing and power.

Basic Jumping Techniques

Approach: Approach the jump at a moderate, controlled speed. Keep your body relaxed and centered over the bike.

Takeoff: As you reach the lip of the jump, compress your legs and arms slightly, then push upwards and slightly forwards.

Mid-Air: Keep your body balanced and level. Look ahead to where you want to land.

Landing: Land with your knees and elbows bent to absorb the impact. Land both wheels simultaneously for a smooth transition.

Example: Mike practiced on tabletop jumps at his local bike park, focusing on maintaining balance and compressing his legs and arms during takeoff.

Advanced Jumping Techniques

Manuals into Jumps: Perform a manual (lifting the front wheel) right before the takeoff to gain extra height and control.

Whips: Twist the bike sideways in the air and bring it back before landing. This adds style and helps with balance.

Example: Emma practiced manualing into jumps to improve her control and experimented with small whips to enhance her technique.

Mastering Switchbacks

Types of Switchbacks

Uphill Switchbacks: Sharp turns on a climb that require precise handling and power control.

Downhill Switchbacks: Sharp turns on a descent that require controlled braking and body position adjustments.

Techniques for Uphill Switchbacks

Body Position: Lean forward to keep the front wheel down and weight your pedals evenly.

Gear Management: Shift to a lower gear before entering the switchback.

Line Choice: Enter wide, cut the apex close, and then exit wide. This smoothens the turn.

Power Application: Apply consistent, smooth power to maintain traction.

Example: Lisa leaned forward and kept her eyes focused through the turn, maintaining steady pedal pressure to navigate uphill switchbacks efficiently.

Techniques for Downhill Switchbacks

Body Position: Shift your weight back slightly, drop your heels, and keep your elbows and knees bent.

Braking: Brake before the turn, then release as you navigate through it. Avoid braking in the middle of the turn to maintain traction.

Line Choice: Enter wide, cut the apex close, and then exit wide, just like uphill switchbacks.

Example: David pre-braked before entering a downhill switchback and used his body position to stay balanced while navigating the turn.

Navigating Rock Gardens

Understanding Rock Gardens

Composition: Filled with various sizes of rocks, requiring precise handling and balance.

Common Challenges: Maintaining traction, choosing the right line, and avoiding mechanical failures.

Techniques for Rock Gardens

Body Position: Stand in the attack position with level pedals, knees, and elbows bent.

Momentum: Keep a steady speed; too slow can cause you to get stuck, and too fast can reduce control.

Line Choice: Look ahead and choose the smoothest line. Avoid large rocks if possible.

Weight Distribution: Keep your weight centered and use your arms and legs as suspension.

Example: Sarah kept her eyes focused ahead while navigating a rock garden, maintaining a steady speed and using her body to absorb impacts.

Fine-Tuning for Rock Gardens

Tire Pressure: Adjust tire pressure for better traction. Slightly lower pressure can improve grip but be cautious of pinch flats.

Suspension Adjustments: Ensure your suspension is set to absorb the impacts effectively.

Example: Mark adjusted his tire pressure and suspension settings for a technical rock garden, finding a balance between traction and control.

Advancing Skills on Technical Trails

Jessica, an advanced rider, sought to enhance her technical riding skills on extreme terrains. She practiced different techniques on familiar trails, focusing on body positioning, line choice, and smooth power application. Jessica also joined an advanced skills clinic, where she received professional guidance on jumping and navigating rock gardens. Through consistent practice and expert tips, Jessica mastered these advanced skills, allowing her to confidently ride complex trails and enjoy a higher level of mountain biking proficiency.

Final Thoughts

Mastering advanced mountain biking skills for handling extreme terrains, performing jumps, navigating switchbacks, and tackling rock gardens significantly enhances your riding experience. By focusing on proper body positioning, line choice, and controlled momentum, you can navigate challenging conditions with confidence and precision. Regular practice and seeking professional guidance through skills clinics can further refine your techniques, allowing you to ride more challenging trails safely and enjoyably.

CHAPTER 22

Seasonal Riding Tips

Can I mountain bike ride in the winter when the ground is muddy? What do I need to know about riding in hot weather?

Mountain biking is an exciting and rewarding sport that can be enjoyed year-round, but each season presents unique challenges and opportunities. Understanding how to adapt your riding techniques, gear, and maintenance practices to different weather conditions will ensure safe and enjoyable rides throughout the year. Here's a detailed guide to help you navigate winter biking, muddy trails, and hot weather riding.

Here we provide advice for riding in different seasons, including winter biking, dealing with mud, and hot weather riding

Winter Biking

Challenges of Winter Biking

Cold Temperatures: Increased risk of hypothermia and frostbite.

Snow and Ice: Reduced traction and higher chances of slips and falls.

Shorter Daylight Hours: Limited riding time and increased need for proper lighting.

Gear and Clothing

Layering: Wear moisture-wicking base layers, insulating mid-layers, and a waterproof, windproof outer layer.

Cold-Weather Accessories: Use thermal gloves, insulated footwear, and a balaclava or face mask to protect extremities.

Example: Emma wears a merino wool base layer, a fleece mid-layer, and a Gore-Tex jacket to stay warm and dry during her winter rides.

Bike Setup

Tires: Use wider, studded tires for better traction on snow and ice.

Brakes: Ensure your brakes work effectively in cold and icy conditions; hydraulic disc brakes often perform better than mechanical ones.

Lubrication: Use a wet or winter-specific chain lube to prevent freezing and ensure smooth operation.

Example: David switches to studded tires and uses a winter-grade chain lube to tackle icy trails.

Riding Techniques

Traction Management: Keep your weight balanced to maintain traction, and avoid sudden movements that could cause slips.

Speed Control: Ride at a controlled speed and approach corners slowly to avoid skidding.

Example: Lisa rides with a steady pace and avoids sharp braking or turns on icy sections to maintain control.

Safety Tips

Visibility: Use bright lights and wear reflective gear to increase visibility in low-light conditions.

Plan Ahead: Know your route, inform someone of your plans, and carry a cellphone for emergencies.

Warm-Up and Cool-Down: Warm up before your ride to prevent injuries and cool down appropriately to avoid sudden temperature changes.

Example: Mark uses a high-lumen light on his handlebars and wears a reflective vest to stay visible during dusk rides.

Riding in Muddy Conditions

Challenges of Muddy Trails

Slippery Surfaces: Increased chances of losing traction.

Trail Damage: Risk of causing erosion and damage to trails.

Muddy Bike Components: Increased wear and tear on the bike.

Gear and Clothing

Waterproof Gear: Wear waterproof rain jackets, pants, and shoe covers to stay dry.

Mudguards: Install mudguards to reduce the amount of mud splashing onto you and your bike.

Example: Sarah uses a waterproof jacket and pants along with clip-on mudguards to manage mud on rainy days.

Bike Setup

Tire Choice: Use tires with aggressive tread patterns to improve grip in muddy conditions.

Drivetrain Maintenance: Clean and lube your drivetrain regularly to prevent mud buildup and ensure smooth shifting.

Example: Tom switches to tires with deeper treads and carries an extra bottle of chain lube to maintain his bike during muddy rides.

Riding Techniques

Pedal Smoothly: Avoid sudden bursts of power that can spin your wheels. Focus on smooth, consistent pedaling.

Body Position: Keep a low center of gravity by bending your knees and elbows. Shift your weight back slightly to maintain traction on climbs.

Example: Emma pedals smoothly and stays centered over her bike to navigate through a muddy forest trail without slipping.

Trail Etiquette

Avoid Sensitive Areas: Stay off trails that are too muddy to prevent excessive damage and erosion.

Stick to Established Trails: Avoid creating new paths, which can cause further environmental damage.

Example: David checks local trail conditions online before heading out and avoids trails that are too wet and likely to suffer damage.

Riding in Hot Weather

Challenges of Hot Weather Riding

Heat Exhaustion and Dehydration: Increased risk of heat-related illnesses.

Overheating: Reduced physical performance due to high temperatures.

Sun Exposure: Increased risk of sunburn and skin damage.

Gear and Clothing

Breathable Clothing: Wear light, moisture-wicking fabrics like synthetic materials or merino wool.

Sun Protection: Use sunscreen, sunglasses, and lightweight, long-sleeve jerseys to protect against UV rays.

Hydration Pack: Carry a hydration pack to ensure you stay hydrated throughout your ride.

Example: Lisa wears a lightweight, long-sleeve jersey and carries a hydration pack to stay cool and protected from the sun.

Bike Setup

Tire Pressure: Lower your tire pressure slightly to improve traction on dry, loose terrain.

Ventilated Helmet: Use a helmet with good ventilation to help keep your head cool.

Example: Mark lowers his tire pressure a bit and switches to a well-ventilated helmet for better performance in hot weather.

Riding Techniques

Pace Yourself: Ride at a moderate pace to avoid overheating. Take breaks in shaded areas to cool down.

Hydration: Drink water regularly, even if you don't feel thirsty. Use electrolyte tablets or drinks to maintain electrolyte balance.

Example: Sarah takes frequent breaks in the shade and sips water regularly to prevent heat exhaustion during her summer rides.

Safety Tips

Ride Early or Late: Avoid the peak heat of the day by riding early in the morning or in the late afternoon.

Know the Symptoms: Be aware of the symptoms of heat exhaustion and heatstroke, and take immediate action if you experience them.

Example: Emma schedules her rides for early morning to beat the heat and reduce the risk of heat-related issues.

Seasonal Riding Adaptation

Jessica, an avid mountain biker, rides year-round by adapting her techniques and gear to different seasonal conditions. In winter, she wears insulated layers and uses studded tires for icy trails. During muddy spring rides, Jessica opts for waterproof gear and aggressive tire treads. In the summer, she prioritizes hydration, wears breathable clothing, and rides early to avoid the peak heat. These adaptations allow Jessica to enjoy mountain biking in any season safely and comfortably.

Final Thoughts

Adapting your mountain biking practices to different seasonal conditions is essential for a safe and enjoyable riding experience. By understanding the challenges and implementing the appropriate gear, bike setup, and riding techniques for winter, muddy conditions, and hot weather, you can ride confidently year-round. Embrace these seasonal tips to make the most of your mountain biking adventures, regardless of the weather.

CHAPTER 23

Women-Specific Riding Tips

I'm a 35 year old female. I've been riding road bikes for several years and have always wanted to try mountain biking. Is it too late for me to take up mountain biking? What do I need to know to get started?

Mountain biking is a thrilling and empowering sport that is gaining popularity among women worldwide. While the fundamental techniques of mountain biking apply to everyone, women may encounter specific challenges and have unique needs. Tailored advice on gear, techniques, community support, and training can significantly enhance the riding experience for female mountain bikers.

Here we provide tailored advice for female mountain bikers, highlighting women-specific gear and communities

Choosing the Right Bike

Women-Specific Bikes

Description: Many manufacturers offer women-specific mountain bikes designed with geometry and components suited to female riders.

Features: Shorter top tubes, narrower handlebars, women-specific saddles, and adjusted suspension settings.

Example: The Liv Pique range is designed specifically for women, offering a tailored fit and performance.

Custom Fitting

Importance: Ensures comfort, efficiency, and control. Consider a professional fitting if a women-specific bike isn't available.

Components to Adjust: Handlebar width, stem length, saddle position, and suspension settings.

Example: Lisa had her bike professionally fitted, adjusting the handlebar width and suspension to match her riding style and body dimensions.

Women-Specific Gear

Clothing

Description: Comfortable, breathable, and supportive clothing designed specifically for women.

Features: Anatomically designed chamois in shorts, high-waistbands, and adjustable jerseys.

Example: Emma prefers riding shorts with a high waistband and a well-padded chamois for long rides.

Bike Seat (Saddle)

Importance: A comfortable and well-fitting saddle is crucial for women, as it accommodates wider hips and reduces discomfort during long rides.

Features: Look for women-specific saddles that provide adequate support without hindering leg movement. A good saddle can significantly improve riding comfort and performance.

Example: Sarah uses a women-specific saddle from Selle Italia, designed to provide comfort and support for wider hips, enhancing her overall riding experience.

Protective Gear

Helmet: Choose a lightweight, well-ventilated helmet—some include women-specific designs with better fit for smaller heads.

Pads and Gloves: Ensure appropriate sizing for knee and elbow pads and gloves.

Example: Sarah uses the POC Tectal helmet, designed for better fit and comfort, alongside women-specific gloves from Fox Racing.

Footwear

Shoes: Consider mountain biking shoes that provide a snug fit, good support, and grip.

Choice of Pedals: Decide between clipless pedals or flat pedals based on comfort and riding style.

Example: Jessica chooses Shimano clipless shoes with a narrower fit for secure and responsive pedaling.

Training and Skill Development

Skill Clinics and Workshops

Importance: Provides structured learning and confidence-building in a supportive environment.

Women-Specific Clinics: Look for women-specific skills clinics that cater to varying skill levels.

Example: Emma attended a women-specific clinic organized by REI, improving her technical skills and gaining confidence.

Mentorship and Guidance

Finding Mentors: Connect with experienced female riders for guidance, tips, and support.

Community Engagement: Join local riding clubs, groups, and online forums for advice and shared experiences.

Example: Lisa joined the Trail Sisters forum, which connected her with experienced female riders who mentored her through her initial mountain biking journey.

Training Programs

Fitness and Conditioning: Focus on strength, endurance, and flexibility training tailored to mountain biking.

Example: Sarah followed a fitness program that included weight training, cardio, and yoga, enhancing her agility and endurance on the trails.

Overcoming Common Challenges

Building Confidence

Regular Practice: Ride regularly to build skills and confidence gradually.

Comfort Zone: Push boundaries incrementally to enhance your capability without compromising safety.

Example: Jessica set a goal to conquer a specific technical trail section each month, building her confidence and skills progressively.

Peer Support

Finding Riding Partners: Connect with other female riders through clubs, events, or social media groups.

Riding Together: Benefit from the encouragement and shared learning experiences of riding with peers.

Example: Emma joined a women's mountain biking group, enjoying the camaraderie and support of fellow female riders on group rides.

Addressing Concerns

Safety: Prioritize safety by wearing appropriate gear and riding within your limits.

Dealing with Fear: Acknowledge fear but approach challenges methodically and with the support of peers or mentors.

Example: Sarah took incremental steps to tackle her fear of descents, starting with gentle slopes and gradually progressing to steeper trails.

Nutrition and Health

Balanced Diet

Nutritional Needs: Maintain a balanced diet rich in protein, carbohydrates, and healthy fats to support energy and recovery.

Hydration: Stay hydrated, especially on long rides and hot days. Use sugar-free electrolyte drinks to maintain balance.

Example: Lisa prepares energy-boosting snacks like beef jerky, nuts and dried fruits for her rides, ensuring sustained energy levels.

Supplements

Specific Needs: Consider supplements like iron and calcium, which may be important for female athletes.

Consultation: Consult with a healthcare professional to tailor supplement needs to individual requirements.

Example: Emma consults with her nutritionist to ensure her diet meets her athletic demands, incorporating supplements like iron for better endurance and calcium for faster muscle recovery.

Building Community and Advocacy

Joining Clubs and Groups

Local Clubs: Join women-specific mountain biking clubs to meet like-minded riders.

Online Communities: Engage in online forums and social media groups to share experiences and get advice.

Example: Sarah joined the Women's MTB Network on Facebook, finding a wealth of resources and networking opportunities. She ended up really connecting with two other women and they have lunch together after their weekly rides.

Supporting Women's Events

Participate and Volunteer: Attend women-specific events like races, clinics, and group rides, and volunteer to support these initiatives.

Example: Lisa volunteered at a women's mountain biking festival, helping to organize clinics and making new connections in the community.

Advocating for Inclusivity

Promote Inclusivity: Advocate for more women in mountain biking through local clubs, trail advocacy groups, and social media.

Example: Jessica started a blog to share her experiences as a female mountain biker, encouraging more women to join the sport.

Women-Specific Events and Races

Participating in Events

Events to Join: Participate in women-specific events like the Grit Clinics and She Rides workshops.

Why Join: Gain skills in a supportive environment and connect with other female riders.

Example: Emma participated in a women's enduro race, finding it a fun and empowering experience.

Races and Competitions

Women-Specific Races: Look for races tailored for female riders, which often offer a supportive and encouraging atmosphere.

Example: Lisa competed in the Beti Bike Bash, a women's-only mountain bike race that celebrated female athletes.

Empowering Journey Through Community Support

Jessica, inspired by seeing more women in mountain biking, decided to get more involved. She attended women-specific clinics to improve her skills and joined local riding groups to meet other female riders. Jessica also volunteered at women's biking events, helping to organize and support new riders. Her involvement transformed her riding experience, providing her with a network of supportive peers, enhancing her skills, and fostering a deep sense of community. Now she celebrates Thanksgiving with her mountain bike friends as well as with her family.

Final Thoughts

Women-specific riding tips, gear, training, and community support play a significant role in enhancing the mountain biking experience for female riders. By choosing the right bike and gear, participating in skill development programs, embracing community support, and advocating for inclusivity, women can navigate the trails confidently and enjoy the sport to its fullest. Embrace these tips and become part of the vibrant and growing community of female mountain bikers.

Youth and Family Biking

How hard is it to introduce kids to mountain biking?
What do I need to know?

Mountain biking is a fantastic activity for families, promoting physical
fitness, outdoor exploration, and quality time together. Engaging young
riders and ensuring family-friendly biking experiences requires proper
preparation, the right equipment, and an understanding of the unique
needs of younger and less experienced riders. Here's a comprehensive
guide to help you introduce your children to mountain biking and enjoy
rewarding family rides.

Here we provide tips for engaging young riders and enjoying family-friendly biking experiences

Choosing the Right Equipment for Young Riders

Kid-Specific Bikes

Description: Bikes designed for children, taking into account their size, strength, and skill level.

Features: Lightweight frames, child-specific geometry, and components suited for smaller hands and legs.

Example: The Trek Precaliber series offers kid-specific mountain bikes with adjustable components to grow with the child.

Proper Bike Fit

Importance: Ensures comfort, control, and safety. Make sure the bike fits well, allowing the child to reach the pedals and handlebars comfortably.

Adjustments: Saddle height, handlebar reach, and brake lever adjustments are crucial for a proper fit.

Example: Tom adjusted his son's bike saddle and handlebar to ensure a comfortable and secure fit, enhancing his riding confidence.

Safety Gear

Helmets: Ensure a well-fitting helmet that covers the forehead and is snug without being tight.

Protective Pads: Consider knee and elbow pads to protect against falls, especially for beginners.

Example: Lisa equipped her daughter with a helmet, knee pads, and gloves, ensuring maximum protection on family rides.

Building Skills and Confidence

Start with Basics

Skill Building: Teach basic skills like balancing, braking, and pedaling on flat, smooth surfaces before moving to trails.

Practice Sessions: Dedicate time to practice sessions in a park or safe area to build foundational skills.

Example: Emma spent several weekends in a local park teaching her son to balance and brake, building his confidence for trail riding.

Progress Gradually

Incremental Challenge: Gradually introduce more challenging terrain as the child's skills improve. Start with easy trails and progress to moderate ones.

Positive Reinforcement: Encourage and praise efforts, building a positive association with mountain biking.

Example: David introduced his children to easy singletrack trails after they mastered basic skills, praising their progress and boosting their confidence.

Riding Techniques for Kids

Body Position: Teach young riders to maintain a neutral body position with slightly bent knees and elbows for better control.

Braking: Emphasize the importance of controlled braking, using both front and rear brakes to stop smoothly.

Example: Sarah practiced braking drills with her children, helping them understand how to stop safely and efficiently.

Planning Family-Friendly Rides

Choosing Family-Friendly Trails

Trail Selection: Look for trails that are suitable for beginners and families—wide, flat trails without technical features.

Local Parks and Bike Paths: Many local parks and recreational areas offer family-friendly biking paths.

Example: Mark chose a local bike path with gentle grades and scenic views for his family's first trail ride.

Ride Duration and Breaks

Short Rides: Keep initial rides short to match the stamina and interest levels of young riders.

Frequent Breaks: Plan for frequent breaks to rest, hydrate, snack, and enjoy the surroundings.

Example: Lisa planned a 30-minute ride with several stops for snacks and photo opportunities, keeping the experience enjoyable for her children.

Bring Snacks and Plenty of Water

Snacks: Kids get hungry faster than adults and are not able to maintain their emotions when they get hungry. Nothing is worse than being far from home with unhappy, hungry kids. Bring snacks and be sure to offer them around during frequent breaks.

Water: Our kids always wore their own hydration pack and we encouraged them to drink more water at every break. We also encouraged them to "nature pee" on a tree or behind a bush every time we stopped.

Example: Melissa and Sean plan a route with the kids with planned stopping points in pretty yet private locations where they can snack in the shade and the kids can relieve themselves behind a bush if needed. Melissa carries hand sanitizer, toilet paper, paper towels and a couple of zip lock bags so she is prepared for any clean-up that may be necessary after the kids eat or go to the bathroom.

Engaging Activities

Scavenger Hunts: Incorporate scavenger hunts or nature exploration to make rides more interactive and fun.

Local Bike Park with Kids Pump Track: Often cities will have a bike park with a pump track specifically for kids. These are great places to stop by during a family ride so everyone can have fun going over small jumps and around bermed corners while they are developing important skills.

Education: Teach children about local flora, fauna, and trail etiquette during rides.

Example: Emma organized a scavenger hunt for her kids during a trail ride, making the experience educational and exciting.

Ensuring Safety and Preparedness

Essential Gear for Every Ride

First Aid Kit: Carry a basic first aid kit to handle minor injuries like scrapes and cuts.

Hydration and Snacks: Bring plenty of water and healthy snacks to keep energy levels up.

Example: David packed a first aid kit, water bottles, and healthy snacks for a family trail ride, ensuring they were prepared for any situation.

Communication and Supervision

Walkie-Talkies: Use walkie-talkies to maintain communication with older children who may ride ahead.

Supervision: Always supervise young riders closely, especially on unfamiliar or challenging trails.

Example: Sarah used walkie-talkies to stay connected with her older children during a family ride, ensuring everyone stayed together and safe.

Trail Etiquette and Respect

Teach Etiquette: Educate children on trail etiquette, such as yielding to other trail users, not littering, and respecting nature.

Respect Wildlife: Remind children to observe wildlife from a distance and not disturb their habitats.

Example: Mark taught his kids to yield to hikers and avoid disturbing wildlife, instilling respect and responsibility.

Encouraging Regular Participation

Consistency and Routine

Regular Rides: Schedule regular family rides to build routine and enthusiasm.

Special Events: Participate in family biking events or organized rides to keep motivation high.

Example: Lisa planned bi-weekly family rides, making it a fun, anticipated activity for everyone.

Celebrate Achievements

Milestones: Celebrate biking milestones like completing a challenging trail or mastering a new skill.

Fun Rewards: Use fun rewards like a picnic or a visit to a favorite spot to celebrate achievements.

Example: Emma celebrated her son's first successful ride on a moderate trail with a picnic at his favorite park.

Introducing Friends and Social Rides

Group Rides: Organize rides with family friends and their children to make biking a social activity.

Community Events: Join community biking events for families, fostering friendships and shared experiences.

Example: Sarah organized a group ride with family friends, making the experience more enjoyable and social for her children.

Creating Positive Experiences

Focusing on Fun

Enjoyment: Emphasize the fun and adventurous aspects of mountain biking, rather than focusing solely on skills and fitness.

Family Bonding: Use biking as an opportunity to bond as a family, sharing the joy of outdoor exploration.

Example: Mark focused on making rides fun, with games and storytelling, ensuring his kids associated biking with positive experiences.

Special Outings and Adventures

Weekend Trips: Plan special weekend biking trips to explore new trails and create memorable experiences.

Adventure Challenges: Set up adventure challenges like finding the tallest tree or the most colorful rock during rides.

Example: David planned a weekend trip to a nearby national park, where the family explored new trails and enjoyed a camping adventure.

Introducing Kids to Mountain Biking

Jessica, an enthusiastic mountain biker and mother of two, wanted to share her passion for biking with her children. She started by teaching them basic skills in a local park, progressing to gentle trails as their confidence grew. Jessica ensured they had the right gear, including well-fitting helmets and protective pads. She organized trips to the bike park and educational activities during trail rides to keep them engaged. The family established a routine of weekend rides, celebrating milestones and creating lasting memories. Jessica's approach made mountain biking a cherished family activity, fostering a love for the sport in her children.

Final Thoughts

Engaging young riders and enjoying family-friendly biking experiences is a rewarding endeavor that brings families closer while promoting physical activity and a love for the outdoors. By choosing the right equipment, building skills and confidence, planning engaging rides, ensuring safety, and creating positive experiences, you can make mountain biking a fun and enjoyable family activity. Embrace these tips and enjoy the countless benefits of family mountain biking adventures.

CHAPTER 25

First Aid and Safety

What do I need to know about handling emergencies out in the woods? What kind of problems may I run into while out mountain biking?

Mountain biking is an exhilarating sport and it comes with inherent risks that can lead to various injuries. While injuries don't happen often, being prepared with basic first aid knowledge and safety tips is essential for ensuring that injuries are managed effectively, reducing the severity of incidents, and promoting a safe riding environment. Here's a comprehensive guide to first aid techniques and safety tips for common injuries you might encounter on the trail.

Here we cover basic first aid techniques and safety tips for dealing with common injuries on the trail

Common Mountain Biking Injuries

Scrapes and Abrasions

Description: Surface wounds caused by sliding or falling on rough terrain.

First Aid: Clean the wound with water and apply an antiseptic. Cover with a sterile dressing or adhesive bandage.

Example: Sarah fell on a rocky section, scraping her arm. She cleaned the wound with her water bottle, applied antiseptic, and covered it with a bandage from her first aid kit.

Cuts and Lacerations

Description: Deeper wounds caused by sharp objects like rocks or branches.

First Aid: Apply pressure to stop bleeding. Clean the wound with antiseptic and cover it with a sterile bandage. Seek medical attention if the cut is deep or doesn't stop bleeding.

Example: Mark cut his leg on a sharp rock. He applied firm pressure to the wound, cleaned it thoroughly, and dressed it with a sterile bandage.

Bruises

Description: Discoloration and pain caused by trauma to the skin and underlying tissues.

First Aid: Apply a cold pack to reduce swelling and relieve pain. Elevate the bruised area if possible.

Example: Lisa bruised her thigh in a minor fall. She applied a cold pack from her first aid kit to reduce swelling.

Sprains and Strains

Description: Injuries to ligaments (sprains) or muscles (strains) resulting from overextension or impact.

First Aid: Follow the RICE method—Rest, Ice, Compression, Elevation. Use a compression bandage and seek medical attention if necessary.

Example: Tom sprained his ankle after misjudging a jump. He followed the RICE method, using an elastic bandage and elevating his foot.

Fractures

Description: Broken bones resulting from high-impact falls or collisions.

First Aid: Immobilize the affected area using a splint or improvised support. Avoid moving the injured person and seek immediate medical assistance.

Example: Emma suspected a fracture in her forearm after a fall. Her friends used a stick and a bandana to create a splint and called for emergency help.

Essential First Aid Kit Contents

Basic Kit Items

1. Adhesive Bandages: Various sizes for minor cuts and abrasions.

2. Sterile Gauze Pads and Dressings: For covering larger wounds and lacerations.

3. Antiseptic Wipes or Solution: For cleaning wounds and preventing infection.

4. Medical Tape: For securing dressings and splints.

5. Elastic Bandage: For compression in case of sprains and strains.

6. Cold Pack: For reducing swelling and relieving pain.

7. Scissors and Tweezers: For cutting bandages and removing debris from wounds.

8. Pain Relievers: Over-the-counter options like ibuprofen or acetaminophen.

Example: Mark carries a well-stocked first aid kit with all the essential items, ensuring he's prepared for common trail injuries.

Additional Items

1. Medical Gloves: For hygienic wound care.

2. Splint Material: Small, foldable splints for immobilizing fractures.

3. Emergency Blanket: For maintaining body warmth in case of shock or hypothermia.

Example: Sarah adds an emergency blanket and medical gloves to her first aid kit, preparing for more serious emergencies.

First Aid Techniques for Common Injuries

Wound Cleaning and Dressing

Procedure: Clean the wound gently with water to remove dirt and debris. Apply antiseptic to prevent infection. Cover with a sterile dressing or bandage.

Example: Tom cleaned his scraped knee with water, applied antiseptic, and covered it with a sterile dressing to protect against infection.

Managing Bleeding

Procedure: Apply direct pressure with a clean cloth or gauze pad. Elevate the affected area if possible. Once bleeding stops, clean and dress the wound.

Example: Mark applied direct pressure to a deep cut on his forearm, elevating his arm until the bleeding stopped before dressing the wound.

Immobilizing Fractures

Procedure: Use a splint or rigid support to immobilize the broken bone. Secure with medical tape or bandages. Avoid moving the injured person if the fracture is severe.

Example: Lisa used a stick and her belt to create an improvised splint for a suspected fractured wrist, stabilizing it until professional help arrived.

Treating Sprains and Strains

Procedure: Follow the RICE method—Rest the injured part, apply Ice to reduce swelling, use Compression with an elastic bandage, and Elevate the limb above heart level.

Example: Emma applied the RICE method to her sprained ankle, using an elastic bandage and elevating her foot to manage swelling and pain.

Handling Head Injuries

Procedure: If a rider hits their head, monitor for signs of concussion such as dizziness, confusion, or unconsciousness. Seek immediate medical attention if symptoms are severe.

Example: Sarah hit her head in a fall but felt fine initially. However, she kept an eye on symptoms and sought medical attention when she experienced a persistent headache and dizziness.

General Safety Tips

Pre-Ride Preparation

Route Planning: Know the trail and plan your route. Share your plans with someone who is not riding with you.

Check Weather Conditions: Ensure you're aware of weather forecasts and prepare accordingly.

Bike Inspection: Perform a pre-ride inspection, checking tire pressure, brakes, and suspension.

Example: Tom plans his ride by checking the trail map, weather forecast, and performing a quick bike inspection to ensure everything is in working order.

Riding Safely

Wear Protective Gear: Always wear a helmet, gloves, and other protective gear.

Ride Within Your Limits: Know your skill level and avoid attempting trails or stunts beyond your ability.

Stay Alert: Be aware of your surroundings and anticipate obstacles.

Example: Lisa stays alert and avoids risky sections beyond her skill level, prioritizing safety over challenge.

Communication and Navigation

Use GPS Devices: Carry a GPS device or smartphone with a trail map app.

Communication Tools: Carry a fully charged phone and consider walkie-talkies for group rides.

Example: Emma uses a GPS device to navigate new trails and carries a phone for emergencies.

Group Riding

Stick Together: When riding in a group, ensure no one gets left behind.

Regular Check-Ins: Stop periodically to check in with all riders, ensuring everyone is safe and accounted for.

Example: Mark leads group rides, taking regular breaks to check in with each rider and ensure no one is struggling.

Emergency Preparedness

Emergency Contacts

Have a Plan: Know who to contact in case of an emergency, including local emergency services and personal contacts.

Example: Sarah keeps a list of emergency contacts and local emergency service numbers stored in her phone and first aid kit.

Location Sharing and Tracking

Use Location Apps: Use apps that allow real-time location sharing with friends or family members.

Example: Emma uses a location-sharing app during solo rides, allowing her friends to track her location in real-time.

Evacuation Plan

Know Exit Routes: Familiarize yourself with exit routes and access points on the trail in case a quick evacuation is necessary.

Example: David checks the trail map for access points and exit routes before starting his ride, preparing for any unexpected emergencies.

Handling a Mid-Trail Injury

Jessica was riding with friends when one of them fell and sustained a deep cut on their leg. She immediately applied pressure to stop the bleeding, cleaned the wound with antiseptic wipes, and dressed it with sterile gauze from her first aid kit. Jessica used her phone to contact emergency services and provided them with their exact location using a GPS app. The quick and calm response ensured that her friend received professional medical help promptly, and the injury was managed effectively.

Final Thoughts

First aid and safety knowledge are essential for every mountain biker. By being prepared with a well-stocked first aid kit, knowing basic first aid techniques, and implementing general safety practices, you can manage common injuries and ensure a safer riding experience. Embrace these tips to ride confidently and responsibly, prepared to handle any challenges that come your way on the trail.

CHAPTER 26

Traveling with Your Bike

I love my bike and I want to take it with me when I go on a bike tour through Europe. How hard will it be for me to get it there? Is it worth it?

Traveling with your mountain bike can open up a world of exciting riding opportunities, from exploring new trails domestically to embarking on international biking adventures. Whether you're planning a weekend trip to a nearby trail system or an overseas biking holiday, understanding the best practices for safely and legally transporting your bike is essential. Here's a comprehensive guide to help you navigate the logistics of traveling with your bike.

Here are tips for transporting your bike safely and legally, both domestically and internationally

Preparing Your Bike for Travel

Bike Cleaning

Importance: Clean your bike thoroughly before packing it to prevent dirt and grime from damaging components during transit.

Procedure: Use a bike-friendly cleaner, degrease the drivetrain, and rinse off mud and dirt. Dry the bike completely before packing.

Example: Lisa cleaned her bike meticulously, removing all dirt and grime before packing it for her trip to the Rockies.

Inspecting and Servicing

Pre-Travel Check: Inspect your bike for any wear and tear or potential issues. Service critical components like brakes, drivetrain, and suspension.

Example: Tom ensured his bike was in top condition by servicing the brakes and checking the suspension before his biking trip.

Disassembling the Bike

Procedure: Remove the pedals, wheels, and handlebars. Lower or remove the seat post. Secure all components to prevent damage.

Packing Materials: Use bubble wrap, foam tubing, and zip ties to protect delicate parts.

Example: Emma removed the wheels and handlebars, wrapped delicate parts in bubble wrap, and secured everything in her bike case.

Packing and Transporting Your Bike

Bike Cases and Bags

Hard Cases: Provide superior protection but can be heavy and may incur additional airline fees.

Soft Cases: Lightweight and easier to handle, but require careful packing to ensure protection.

Example: Sarah chose a hard case for her international trip to ensure maximum protection during air travel.

Packing the Bike

Securing the Frame: Place the frame in the case, padding it with foam or cardboard to prevent movement.

Wheels and Components: Pack the wheels on either side of the frame, ensuring they are secure. Use separate compartments or padding for smaller components.

Example: Mark placed his bike frame in the center of his case, padded with foam, and secured the wheels in side compartments to prevent shifting.

Labeling and Documentation

Labels: Attach labels with your contact information to the bike case.

Documentation: Carry necessary documents like purchase receipts, travel insurance, and airline regulations concerning bike transport.

Example: Lisa labeled her bike case with her name and contact information and carried a copy of her bike's purchase receipt as proof of ownership.

Air Travel with Your Bike

Understanding Airline Policies

Research: Check your airline's policies on bike transport, including size restrictions, weight limits, and fees.

Booking: Inform the airline in advance that you will be traveling with a bike, and confirm any special requirements.

Example: Tom researched his airline's bike transport policy and booked his bike as checked baggage, factoring in any additional fees.

At the Airport

Check-In: Arrive early to allow extra time for check-in and bike handling procedures.

Handling Fees: Be prepared to pay any applicable bike transport fees at the check-in counter.

Example: Sarah arrived at the airport early, checked in her bike as over-sized baggage, and paid the handling fee, ensuring a smooth process.

Customs and Regulations

International Travel: Be aware of import regulations, duties, and prohibited items related to bike transport in your destination country.

Documentation: Carry necessary documents like purchase receipts and travel insurance to facilitate customs clearance.

Example: Emma checked the import regulations for her destination and ensured she had all required documentation to avoid complications at customs.

Car Travel with Your Bike

Using Bike Racks

Types of Racks: Choose from roof racks, hitch-mounted racks, or trunk racks based on your vehicle and preference.

Installation: Ensure the rack is properly installed and secure before loading your bike.

Example: Mark used a hitch-mounted rack to transport his bike, ensuring it was securely attached and the bike was stable during the drive.

Securing the Bike

Straps and Locks: Use straps to secure the bike to the rack and locks to prevent theft.

Padding: Use padding to protect your bike from scratches and road debris.

Example: Lisa used foam padding and heavy-duty straps to secure her bike to the roof rack, preventing any movement during the drive.

Interior Transport

Disassembly: Partially disassemble the bike if transporting it inside your vehicle, removing the wheels and seat post as necessary.

Protection: Use blankets or pads to protect both the bike and your vehicle's interior.

Example: Emma disassembled her bike and used blankets to cushion it inside her SUV, ensuring a safe and secure transport.

International Travel Considerations

Travel Insurance

Coverage: Ensure your travel insurance covers bike transport and potential damage or loss during transit.

Proof of Ownership: Carry purchase receipts and detailed photos of your bike for insurance claims if needed.

Example: Tom included his bike in his travel insurance policy and took photos of his bike and its components as proof of ownership.

Destination Research

Local Trails: Research bike-friendly trails and routes in your destination area.

Local Laws: Familiarize yourself with local biking laws and regulations to ensure compliance.

Example: Sarah researched popular trails in her destination country and familiarized herself with local traffic laws for cyclists.

Local Services

Bike Shops: Locate bike shops near your destination for any needed repairs or equipment purchases.

Rentals: Consider renting a bike if transporting your own is impractical or cost-prohibitive.

Example: Lisa located a bike shop near her hotel that offered repair services and rentals, providing peace of mind for her travel plans.

General Tips for Traveling with Your Bike

Packing Checklist

Essentials: Create a checklist of essential items, including bike tools, spare parts, and protective gear.

Packing Order: Organize and pack your gear methodically to ensure nothing is forgotten.

Example: Mark prepared a detailed checklist, ensuring he packed all necessary tools, spare tubes, and his riding gear.

Adapting to Transport Delays

Contingency Plan: Be prepared for potential transport delays or issues with bike handling.

Example: Emma packed a multi-tool and essentials in her carry-on, allowing her to handle minor bike adjustments if needed upon arrival.

Health and Hydration

Stay Hydrated: Drink plenty of water before, during, and after your journey to prevent dehydration.

Stretching: Perform stretching exercises during long journeys to prevent stiffness and discomfort.

Example: Sarah stayed hydrated and took regular breaks to stretch during her road trip to a biking destination.

Smooth Bike Travel Experience

Jessica planned a biking holiday to Europe and needed to ensure her bike arrived safely. She chose a high-quality hard case, carefully disassembled and packed her bike with plenty of padding, and labeled it with her contact information. Jessica arrived at the airport early to manage the check-in process, paid the necessary fees, and carried all required documentation. Upon arrival, her bike was intact, and she could enjoy her European biking adventure without any issues. Her thorough preparation ensured a smooth and stress-free travel experience.

Final Thoughts

Traveling with your bike can be a rewarding and seamless experience with the right preparation and knowledge. By understanding how to disassemble, pack, and transport your bike safely, whether by car or air, and navigating international travel considerations, you can explore new trails and destinations confidently. Embrace these tips to ensure your biking adventures are enjoyable and hassle-free, wherever your travels take you.

CHAPTER 27

Biking Adventures

How do I prepare for multi-day biking expeditions or bikepacking trips?

Preparing for multi-day biking expeditions or bikepacking trips requires careful planning, the right gear, and a solid understanding of your route and conditions. Here are the most important things you need to know to help you get ready:

Route Planning

Research Your Route

How to Use: Study maps, guidebooks, and online resources to understand the terrain, distance, and difficulty of your route.

Example: Use websites like Bikepacking.com and apps like Trailforks to gather detailed information about popular routes.

Plan Your Daily Mileage

How to Use: Determine how many miles you can comfortably ride each day, considering elevation gain and technical difficulty.

Example: For a beginner, planning 30-40 miles per day on moderate terrain is a good starting point.

Identify Campsites and Water Sources

How to Use: Mark potential campsites and water sources along your route.

Example: National parks often have designated campsites, and topographic maps can show rivers and streams.

Packing Essentials

Bikepacking Bags

Types: Use frame bags, handlebar bags, saddle bags, and backpack if necessary to distribute weight evenly.

Example: Revelate Designs offers a range of bikepacking bags designed for different needs and bike frames.

Shelter

Options: Lightweight tent, bivy sack, or hammock with a rainfly.

Example: The Big Agnes Fly Creek HV UL2 is a popular ultralight tent.

Sleeping Gear

Essentials: Sleeping bag rated for expected temperatures and a compact sleeping pad.

Example: Sea to Summit Ultralight Insulated Sleeping Pad and a Marmot Phase 20 Sleeping Bag.

Cooking Equipment

Essentials: Lightweight stove, pot, utensils, and fuel.

Example: MSR PocketRocket stove and a titanium pot.

Food and Water

Food: Pack lightweight, high-calorie foods like dehydrated meals, energy bars, nuts, and dried fruits.

Water: Carry enough water for your ride and a reliable purification method.

Example: A Sawyer Mini water filter is compact and efficient.

Clothing

Layers: Bring moisture-wicking base layers, an insulating layer, and a waterproof jacket.

Example: A merino wool base layer, a down jacket, and a Gore-Tex rain jacket.

Tools and Spare Parts

Essentials: Multi-tool, tire levers, spare tubes, chain links, pump, and a small repair kit.

Example: Lezyne multi-tool with integrated chain breaker.

Bike Setup and Maintenance

Pre-Trip Bike Check

Inspection: Thoroughly inspect and service your bike before the trip. Check the drivetrain, brakes, tires, and suspension.

Example: Make sure your tires have enough tread for the terrain and carry fresh sealant if using tubeless tires.

Comfort Adjustment:

Fit: Ensure your bike is properly fitted to reduce discomfort on long rides. Adjust saddle height, handlebar position, and suspension settings.

Example: Consider using ergonomic grips and a comfortable saddle like the Brooks Cambium.

Physical and Mental Preparation

Training

Endurance: Build up your stamina with long rides and back-to-back training days.

Strength: Work on core strength to handle the loaded bike and varied terrain.

Example: Follow a training plan that includes both riding and off-bike exercises like squats and planks.

Mental Preparation

Resilience: Be prepared for challenges like weather changes, mechanical issues, and navigating unfamiliar terrain.

Example: Practice problem-solving and staying calm under pressure during shorter trips.

Preparing for the Great Divide Route

Emily planned a multi-day bikepacking trip on the Great Divide Mountain Bike Route. She researched the route thoroughly, identifying campsites and water sources. Emily packed her Revelate Designs bags with essential gear, including a lightweight tent, sleeping bag, and cooking equipment. She also carried tools and spare parts for potential repairs. To prepare physically, Emily followed a rigorous training plan, incorporating long rides and strength training. The preparation paid off as she navigated the challenging route, enjoying the adventure and overcoming obstacles with confidence.

Final Thoughts

Successfully preparing for multi-day biking expeditions or bikepacking trips involves careful route planning, packing the right gear, ensuring your bike is in top condition, and building physical and mental resilience. By addressing each aspect thoroughly, you can enjoy your adventure with confidence and tackle the challenges that come your way. The preparation enhances the overall experience, making your journey memorable and fulfilling.

CHAPTER 28

Epic Places to Ride

What are some of the most exciting mountain biking destinations around the world?

Exploring new and exciting mountain biking destinations can take your riding experience to the next level. Here are some of the most renowned mountain biking destinations around the world:

Whistler, British Columbia, Canada

Whistler Mountain Bike Park

Description: Known as the mecca of mountain biking, Whistler offers an extensive network of professionally maintained trails suitable for all skill levels.

Must-Ride Trails: "A-Line" for its iconic jumps and flow, and "Crank It Up" for intermediate riders seeking thrills.

Lost Lake Trails

Description: A less intense alternative to the bike park, offering scenic and well-maintained cross-country trails.

Example: Trails like "Jersey Shore" provide forested singletrack and beautiful lake views.

Moab, Utah, USA

Slickrock Trail

Description: Famous for its challenging slickrock terrain and breathtaking desert scenery.

Must-Ride Sections: The main loop is 10.5 miles of heart-pumping climbs and descents.

The Whole Enchilada

Description: A legendary descent that takes you from the La Sal Mountains down to the Colorado River.

Must-Ride Sections: "Burro Pass" for high-altitude, technical riding.

Rotorua, New Zealand

Redwoods Whakarewarewa Forest

Description: Features a diverse range of trails through stunning redwood forests.

Must-Ride Trails: "Billy T" for flowing singletrack and "Tuhoto Ariki" for downhill thrills.

Skyline Rotorua Gravity Park

Description: A lift-accessed bike park offering gravity trails and jump lines.

Must-Ride Trails: "Huckleberry Hound" for fun berms and jumps.

Alps, France

Les Gets Bike Park

Description: Part of the Portes du Soleil region, this park offers a variety of lift-accessed trails.

Must-Ride Trails: "Chavannes" for smooth flow and "Dans Le Gaz" for a steep descent.

Morzine

Description: Known for its technical downhill trails and stunning alpine scenery.

Must-Ride Trails: "Pleney" for classic downhill runs and "Super Morzine" for varied terrain.

Squamish, British Columbia, Canada

Alice Lake and Diamond Head

Description: Offers technical singletrack and stunning sea-to-sky views.

Must-Ride Trails: "Half Nelson" for flowy descents and "Entrails" for technical challenges.

Valleycliffe

Description: A network of trails with technical rock features and fast descents.

Must-Ride Trails: "Rocks and Roots" for technical riding.

Tuscany, Italy

Elba Island

Description: Offers a mix of coastal and mountainous trails with spectacular views.

Must-Ride Trails: "Capoliveri Bike Park" for its diverse terrain and scenic beauty.

Abetone

Bike Park

Description: Part of the Apennine Mountains, offering lift-accessed downhill trails.

Must-Ride Trails: "Rock Oh" for technical descents.

Åre, Sweden

Åre Bike Park

Description: Scandinavia's largest bike park with a variety of downhill and cross-country trails.

Must-Ride Trails: "Million Dollar View" for stunning scenery and "MTB Arena" for challenging downhill runs.

St. Olav's Trail

Description: A historical pilgrim route offering a mix of technical and scenic trails.

Must-Ride Sections: The route passing through Jämtland for a mix of natural beauty and cultural heritage.

Nelson, New Zealand

Codgers Mountain Bike Park

Description: Known for its technical singletrack and scenic vistas.

Must-Ride Trails: "Sunshine Ridge" for a mix of technical sections and flow.

Silvan Forest

Description: Offers a variety of trails that range from easy rides to technical challenges.

Must-Ride Trails: "Involution" for challenging climbs and thrilling descents.

Exploring Whistler

James, an avid mountain biker, planned a trip to Whistler, British Columbia. He spent days exploring Whistler Mountain Bike Park, tackling famous trails like "A-Line" and "Crank It Up."

Because of conditions, he actually found that his favorite trails on the Fitzsimmons part of the mountain were Upper and Lower "Crank it Up". However, his very favorite trail was above in the Garbanzo Zone and was called "Blue Velvet". The park's well-maintained trails and stunning mountain scenery made it a thrilling experience.

James also rode all of the scenic cross-country trails in Lost Lake. He especially liked "Pinocchio's Furniture" which had fun wooden "skinnys". The entire trail system providing a wonderful balance between challenging rides and relaxing scenic tours. The ten day adventure not only enhanced his skills but also left him with unforgettable memories.

Final Thoughts

Exploring renowned mountain biking destinations around the world offers unique experiences and challenges that can enrich your riding journey. Whether you prefer technical descents, flowing singletrack, or multi-day adventures, there are destinations that cater to all tastes and skill levels. Planning trips to these iconic locations allows you to experience different terrains, cultures, and communities, making your passion for mountain biking even more rewarding and diverse.

CHAPTER 29

Staying Up with the Latest Trends and Advancements

How can I stay up-to-date with the latest trends and advancements in mountain biking?

Staying up-to-date with the latest trends and advancements in mountain biking ensures that you are informed about new technologies, techniques, and community developments. Here's how you can keep yourself updated:

Subscribe to Magazines and Newsletters

Mountain Biking Magazines

How to Use: Subscribe to popular mountain biking magazines that provide news, reviews, and features.

Example: Magazines like "Mountain Bike Action" and "Bike Magazine" offer print and digital subscriptions with in-depth articles.

Online Newsletters

How to Use: Sign up for newsletters from biking websites, blogs, and organizations to receive updates directly in your inbox.

Example: Subscribe to the IMBA or Pinkbike newsletters for regular updates on industry news and events.

Follow Social Media Accounts and Forums

Social Media Platforms

How to Use: Follow mountain biking brands, magazines, and influencers on platforms like Instagram, Facebook, and Twitter.

Example: Follow accounts like @bike, @singletracksMTB, and @imba-canada for the latest posts on gear, trails, and events.

Online Forums and Groups

How to Use: Join online forums and groups where riders discuss trends, share tips, and post news.

Example: Engage with communities on Reddit (r/mountainbiking) or MTBR forums.

Attend Industry Events and Expos

Bike Shows and Expos

How to Use: Attend major bike shows and expos to see the latest gear, meet industry experts, and participate in workshops.

Example: Events like the "Sea Otter Classic" and "Interbike" showcase the newest products and innovations.

Engage with YouTube Channels and Podcasts

YouTube Channels

How to Use: Subscribe to YouTube channels that focus on mountain biking content, including gear reviews, tutorials, and vlogs.

Example: Channels like "Seth's Bike Hacks" and "GMBN" (Global Mountain Bike Network) provide a wealth of information and entertainment.

Podcasts

How to Use: Listen to podcasts featuring discussions on the latest trends, interviews with industry leaders, and biking tips.

Example: Subscribe to podcasts like "The Inside Line" by Vital MTB and "MTB Podcast" for engaging and informative content.

Participate in Local and Online Workshops

Skill Clinics

How to Use: Attend local skill clinics and workshops to learn about the latest riding techniques and technologies.

Example: Look for clinics offered by local bike shops or organizations like REI.

Webinars and Online Courses

How to Use: Enroll in webinars and online courses that cover various aspects of mountain biking, from maintenance to advanced riding skills.

Example: IMBA and other organizations often offer webinars on trail building, advocacy, and riding techniques.

Connect with Brands and Manufacturers

Brand Newsletters

How to Use: Subscribe to newsletters from bike brands and manufacturers to receive updates on new products and innovations.

Example: Sign up for newsletters from brands like Trek, Specialized, and Santa Cruz.

Demo Days

How to Use: Participate in demo days organized by bike brands to test new gear and get firsthand knowledge from company representatives.

Example: Attend demo events at local bike shops or trailheads where brands showcase their latest models.

> ### Staying Informed in Colorado
>
> Mike, a dedicated mountain biker from Colorado, stays updated by subscribing to "Mountain Bike Action" magazine and following @pinkbike on Instagram. He attends the "Sea Otter Classic" annually, where he explores new gear and meets industry experts. Mike also listens to the "MTB Podcast" during his daily commute, gaining insights into the latest trends and product reviews. This multi-faceted approach keeps him well-informed and excited about new advancements in the sport.

Final Thoughts

Staying up-to-date with the latest trends and advancements in mountain biking enhances your knowledge and keeps you engaged with the sport. By subscribing to magazines, following social media, attending events, engaging with online content, and connecting with brands, you'll be well-informed about the latest developments. This continuous learning not only improves your riding experience but also deepens your connection with the mountain biking community.

All About Electric Assist Mountain Biking on e-MTBs

All About Electric Assist Mountain Biking on e-MTBs

Electric assist mountain bikes (e-MTB's) are becoming increasingly popular because they extend the timeframe in which people enjoy mountain bike riding. More women are getting into mountain biking or continuing to ride because they are able to enjoy riding and keep up. People of all ages that are managing physical limitations or have injuries appreciate e-MTB's so they can get out into nature.

We are dedicating a third of this book to questions people ask about electric assist mountain bikes because people interested in e-MTB's want to understand the unique aspects of riding and maintaining these bikes.

Here Is What We Will Cover In This Section

Introduction to e-MTBs

- What are e-MTBs, and how do they differ from traditional mountain bikes?

- What types of electric assist systems are available, and how do they work?

Purchasing Guidance

- How do I choose the right e-MTB for my needs and riding style?

- What should I look for in terms of battery life, motor power, and overall bike specifications?

Battery and Charging

- How long does the battery last, and what factors influence its lifespan?

- What are the best practices for charging and storing the battery to maximize its lifespan?

- How do I know when it's time to replace the battery?

Legal and Trail Access

- What are the legal regulations regarding e-MTBs on trails?

- Which trails are e-MTB friendly, and are there specific trail etiquette rules for e-MTB riders?

Riding Techniques

- How do I manage the additional weight and power of an e-MTB on technical trails?

- What specific handling techniques should I adopt for uphill and downhill riding with an e-MTB?

Maintenance and Repairs

- How do I maintain the electric components, such as the motor and battery?

- What are the common issues with e-MTBs, and how can I troubleshoot them?

- Are there specific tools needed for e-MTB maintenance and repairs?

Fitness and Health

- How can e-MTBs be used to improve fitness while reducing physical strain?

- What are the health benefits of using an e-MTB compared to a traditional mountain bike?

Technology and Connectivity

- What smart features are available on modern e-MTBs, and how can I use them effectively?

- How do I integrate my e-MTB with cycling apps and other digital tools for an enhanced riding experience?

Sustainable Practices

- How do e-MTBs contribute to sustainable transportation and recreation?

- What environmental considerations should I keep in mind when using an e-MTB?

Community and Culture

- How do I connect with other e-MTB riders and clubs?

- What are the latest trends and advancements in e-MTB technology and culture?

Performance Optimization

- How can I optimize the performance and range of my e-MTB during rides?

- What techniques can I use to balance the use of pedal power and electric assist for maximum efficiency?

Accessibility

- How can e-MTBs make mountain biking more accessible for riders with physical limitations?

- What adaptive features or accessories are available for e-MTBs?

Safety Concerns

- How do the speed and power of an e-MTB affect safety considerations on the trail?

- What additional safety gear might be necessary for e-MTB riding?

Versatility

- How can I use my e-MTB for multiple purposes, such as commuting, recreational riding, and bikepacking?

- What should I consider when transitioning from trail riding to urban or utility use?

Battery Upgrades

- Are there options for upgrading the battery or motor on my e-MTB?

- What are the cost and performance implications of such upgrades?

CHAPTER 30

Introduction to e-MTBs

What are e-MTBs, and how do they differ from traditional mountain bikes?

Electric assist mountain bikes (e-MTBs) have revolutionized the world of mountain biking, making the sport more accessible and enjoyable for a wider range of riders. Understanding what e-MTBs are and how they differ from traditional mountain bikes is crucial for anyone looking to explore this exciting category. Let's delve into the specifics.

What are e-MTBs?

Electric assist mountain bikes, commonly referred to as e-MTBs, are bicycles equipped with an integrated electric motor that provides pedal assistance to the rider. The motor is powered by a rechargeable battery, and the level of assistance can typically be adjusted through a control system mounted on the handlebars.

Key Components of an e-MTB

Motor

Types: Mid-drive motors (mounted at the bike's crankset) and hub-drive motors (mounted in the rear wheel hub).

Function: The motor assists the rider's pedaling, making it easier to climb hills, accelerate, and maintain speed on various terrains.

Battery

Placement: Often mounted on the down tube, though it can also be integrated into the frame.

Function: Stores electrical energy to power the motor. Battery capacity is measured in watt-hours (Wh), with higher capacities providing longer range.

Controller

Display: Mounted on the handlebars, showing information like speed, battery level, and assistance mode.

Mode Selection: Allows the rider to choose different levels of motor assistance, typically ranging from eco (low assistance) to turbo (high assistance).

Sensors

Torque Sensor: Measures the force applied to the pedals to regulate motor assistance.

Speed Sensor: Measures the bike's speed to ensure assistance is provided appropriately.

Differences Between e-MTBs and Traditional Mountain Bikes

Understanding the differences is essential to appreciate the unique benefits and challenges of riding an e-MTB.

Pedal Assistance

e-MTBs: Provide adjustable pedal assistance, enhancing the rider's pedaling power. This assistance is particularly useful for climbing steep hills, accelerating, and maintaining speed on difficult terrains.

Traditional MTBs: Rely solely on the rider's physical strength and endurance for all pedaling effort.

Weight

e-MTBs: Generally heavier due to the motor, battery, and additional components. The extra weight can affect handling, especially on technical trails.

Traditional MTBs: Lighter, offering more nimble handling and easier maneuverability on technical sections.

Range and Distance

e-MTBs: Can cover longer distances with less fatigue, thanks to motor assistance. The range depends on battery capacity, assistance level, rider weight, and terrain.

Traditional MTBs: The range is limited by the rider's physical endurance and fitness level.

Maintenance

e-MTBs: Require additional maintenance for the motor and battery. Riders need to ensure regular charging and monitor the condition of electric components.

Traditional MTBs: Maintenance focuses on mechanical components like the drivetrain, brakes, and suspension.

Riding Experience

e-MTBs: Offer a different riding experience, allowing riders to tackle more challenging trails and enjoy climbs that might be too exhausting on a traditional bike. The motor's assistance can make rides less physically demanding and more enjoyable for a broader audience.

Traditional MTBs: Provide a pure, unassisted experience where the rider's fitness is the primary factor in overcoming obstacles and enjoying the ride.

Advantages of e-MTBs

Accessibility

e-MTBs make mountain biking accessible to a wider range of people, including those with physical limitations or lower fitness levels. The pedal assistance allows them to enjoy trails they might not otherwise be able to explore.

Extended Rides

The ability to ride longer distances without excessive fatigue means more time enjoying the trails and less worry about energy depletion.

Climbing Efficiency

Hills and steep climbs become more manageable, allowing riders to explore more varied terrains and challenging routes.

Group Rides

e-MTBs can level the playing field in group rides, allowing riders of different fitness levels to ride together without leaving anyone behind.

Challenges of e-MTBs

Weight

The added weight of the motor and battery can make handling more challenging, especially on technical trails and during lift-assisted riding.

Cost

e-MTBs are generally more expensive than traditional mountain bikes, reflecting the added technology and components.

Maintenance

Additional maintenance is required for the electric components, including charging the battery and monitoring the motor and sensors.

Jane's e-MTB Experience

Jane, a 45-year-old avid mountain biker from Colorado, found that her fitness levels started to decline due to a demanding job and limited time for training. She decided to invest in an e-MTB to continue enjoying the challenging trails she loved. With her new e-MTB, Jane was able to ride longer distances, conquer steep climbs with ease, and participate in group rides without feeling left behind. The motor assistance allowed her to maintain her passion for mountain biking despite her busy schedule and reduced fitness. Her experience with the e-MTB opened up new possibilities for exploration and enjoyment.

Final Thoughts

Electric assist mountain bikes are a game-changer in the world of mountain biking. They offer unique benefits that make the sport more accessible, enjoyable, and less physically demanding. By understanding what e-MTBs are and how they differ from traditional mountain bikes, riders can make informed decisions about their cycling adventures. The blend of technology and biking creates new opportunities for riders of all levels to explore trails and experience the thrill of mountain biking in a whole new way.

CHAPTER 31

Purchasing Guidance

How do I choose the right e-MTB for my needs and riding style?

Choosing the right electric assist mountain bike (e-MTB) can be a daunting task given the multitude of options available on the market. The key to making an informed purchase lies in understanding your specific needs, riding style, and the features that best suit these requirements. Here's a comprehensive guide to help you navigate the buying process and select the perfect e-MTB.

Identify Your Riding Style

Cross-Country (XC)

Description: XC riding involves long-distance rides over varied terrain, often including both climbs and descents.

Ideal e-MTB Features: Look for a lightweight e-MTB with efficient pedaling, long range battery, moderate suspension travel (minimum 100-120mm), and a balanced geometry for endurance and efficiency.

Example: The Specialized Turbo Levo SL Comp is a lightweight, agile e-MTB suitable for XC riding.

Trail Riding

Description: Trail riding covers a wide range of terrains and obstacles, including moderate technical features, climbs, and descents.

Ideal e-MTB Features: Choose a versatile e-MTB with more suspension travel (120-140mm), a robust frame, and balanced geometry. Prioritize durability and performance across varied terrains.

Example: The Specialized Turbo Levo Comp Alloy offers balanced performance and durability for trail riding.

All-Mountain/Enduro

Description: All-mountain/enduro riding involves challenging technical descents and steep climbs on rugged terrain.

Ideal e-MTB Features: Opt for an e-MTB with ample suspension travel (150-170mm), a sturdy frame, and aggressive geometry for stability. Look for high-end components that can withstand intense use.

Example: The Santa Cruz Heckler is designed for aggressive all-mountain and enduro riding with its robust build and powerful motor.

Downhill (DH)

Description: Downhill riding focuses on descending steep, technical trails at high speeds, often featuring jumps, drops, and rough terrain.

Ideal e-MTB Features: Look for maximum suspension travel (180-200mm), a very sturdy frame, and slack geometry. Prioritize strength and control during descents.

Example: The Specialized Turbo Kenevo comes with extensive suspension and rugged construction suitable for downhill riding.

Consider the Motor and Battery

Motor Power and Placement

Mid-Drive Motors: Most common in e-MTBs, mounted at the bike's crankset. They offer better weight distribution and efficiency, making them ideal for off-road use.

Hub-Drive Motors: Mounted in the rear or front hub. Less common in high-end e-MTBs but can be suitable for flatter terrains.

Power Output

Watts (W): Motors typically range from 250W to 750W. Higher wattage provides more assistance but may be subject to local regulations for off-road use.

Battery Capacity

Measured in Watt-Hours (Wh): Common e-MTB batteries range from 400Wh to 700Wh. Higher capacity allows for longer rides but adds weight.

Battery Placement: Integrated batteries provide a cleaner look and better weight distribution, while external batteries are easier to replace and upgrade.

Battery Life and Charging

Range: Factors such as assistance level, terrain, rider weight, and weather affect battery range.

Charging Time: Consider the charging time, which typically ranges from 3-6 hours for a full charge.

Evaluate Bike Geometry and Suspension

Geometry

Trail-Focused Geometry: Balanced head angle (65-67 degrees) and steep seat tube angle for control and comfort on varied terrain.

Aggressive Geometry: Slacker head angle (63-65 degrees) for stability during fast descents and technical sections.

Suspension

Travel: The amount of movement in the suspension. More travel (150-180mm) for rough, technical terrain; less travel (100-140mm) for smoother trails.

Type: Full suspension (both front and rear) for most off-road riding. Hardtail (front suspension only) for XC and less technical trails.

Assess Component Quality

Drivetrain

Single vs. Multiple Chainrings: Single chainring setups are simpler and require less maintenance, ideal for e-MTBs.

Gears: Wide-range cassettes (11or 12-speed) provide flexibility for varied terrains.

Brakes

Hydraulic Disc Brakes: Offer superior stopping power and modulation, essential for controlling the extra weight and speed of an e-MTB.

Tires

Width and Tread: Wider tires (2.4" to 2.8") offer better traction and stability. Aggressive tread patterns provide grip on loose and technical terrain.

Test Ride and Personal Fit

Fit and Comfort

Frame Size: Ensure the frame size matches your height and riding style. Test the fit and make sure you feel comfortable and in control.

Adjustability: Look for adjustable components (seat post, handlebars) to fine-tune your fit.

Test Ride

Ride Experience: Test ride different models to feel the motor response, handling, and overall ride quality. Pay attention to how the bike performs on climbs, descents, and technical sections.

Finding the Perfect e-MTB for Trail Riding

Sarah, an avid trail rider from Oregon, wanted to transition to an e-MTB to extend her rides and tackle steeper climbs. She researched models suitable for trail riding and identified the Trek Powerfly FS 4 as a potential choice. The bike's balanced geometry, 130mm suspension travel, and reliable mid-drive motor made it ideal for her needs. After test riding several models, Sarah found the Powerfly FS 4 provided the perfect combination of comfort, control, battery life and power. She appreciated the additional assistance on long climbs and technical sections, enhancing her overall riding experience.

Final Thoughts

Choosing the right e-MTB involves considering your riding style, evaluating key features like motor power, battery capacity, and suspension, and ensuring a proper fit. By understanding these factors and taking the time to test ride different models, you can find an e-MTB that meets your specific needs and enhances your mountain biking adventures. Investing in the right e-MTB will provide years of enjoyment, allowing you to explore new trails, extend your rides, and tackle challenging terrains with confidence.

CHAPTER 32

All About e-MTB Batteries

How long does the battery last, and what factors influence its lifespan?

The battery is one of the most critical components of an electric assist mountain bike (e-MTB). Understanding how long the battery lasts and the factors influencing its lifespan is essential for ensuring optimal performance and longevity of your e-MTB. Let's delve into the specifics.

Battery Lifespan

The lifespan of an e-MTB battery is typically measured in charge cycles. One charge cycle is defined as one full discharge and recharge of the battery. Most high-quality e-MTB batteries are designed to last between 500 to 1,000 charge cycles, which can translate to several years of regular use. However, the actual lifespan can vary based on several factors:

Type of Battery

Lithium-ion (Li-ion): The most common type used in e-MTBs. They offer a high energy density, long lifespan, and relatively low weight.

Lifespan: With proper care, Li-ion batteries can maintain good performance for 3-5 years or more.

Factors Influencing Battery Lifespan

Charging Practices

Regular Charging: Avoid letting the battery drain completely before recharging. Frequent partial charges can help extend the battery's life.

Overcharging: Modern batteries often have built-in protection, but it's still advisable to disconnect the charger once the battery is fully charged to avoid potential overcharging.

Example: Alex charges his e-MTB battery after every ride, ensuring it's never completely drained. This practice helps maintain the battery's health over time.

Temperature Conditions

Storage Temperature: Store the battery in a cool, dry place when not in use. Extreme temperatures, both hot and cold, can degrade the battery's performance and lifespan.

Operating Temperature: Avoid exposing the battery to very high or low temperatures during rides. Extreme cold can reduce the battery's efficiency, while extreme heat can cause damage.

Example: Keeping the battery in a garage during winter, where temperatures drop below freezing, can negatively impact its lifespan. Sarah stores her battery indoors in a climate-controlled environment to avoid such issues.

Usage Patterns

Assistance Level: Using higher levels of motor assistance drains the battery more quickly. Balancing the use of different assistance levels can help extend the battery's lifespan.

Terrain and Riding Style: Steep climbs, technical terrain, and aggressive riding require more power and can reduce the battery's range and lifespan.

Example: John uses eco mode for flat sections and reserves higher assistance levels for steep climbs, balancing power usage and extending the battery's overall life.

Weight and Load

Rider and Cargo Weight: The more weight the motor has to assist, the more power it consumes. Carrying heavy loads or having a higher body weight can impact the battery's performance.

Example: Lisa, who uses her e-MTB for bikepacking, ensures she packs light and distributes weight evenly to avoid excessive strain on the battery.

Maximizing Battery Performance

To get the most out of your e-MTB battery, follow these best practices:

Charge Regularly and Properly

Follow the manufacturer's guidelines for charging to avoid overcharging and deep discharging.

Example: Tom follows his manual's instructions to charge the battery after each ride and disconnect it once fully charged.

Monitor and Maintain Battery Health

Check battery connections and terminals for corrosion or damage. Clean them gently if necessary.

Example: Emma inspects her battery and keeps the contacts clean and free of dirt and moisture.

Use Protective Gear

Consider using protective covers or cases for the battery to shield it from extreme weather and physical damage.

Example: Mark uses a weatherproof cover for his battery when riding in rainy conditions to prevent moisture damage.

Store Correctly During Inactivity

If you won't be using your e-MTB for an extended period, store the battery at around 50% charge and in a temperature-controlled environment.

Example: During the off-season, Rachel stores her e-MTB battery in her home's cool, dry basement at 50% charge.

Maximizing Battery Life for Daily Commutes

Mike, a daily e-MTB commuter, noticed reduced battery performance after a year of regular use. He revised his charging practices by avoiding full discharges and overcharging. He started storing his battery indoors during extreme weather and used protective covers during rides in adverse conditions. By balancing his usage patterns and maintaining his battery regularly, Mike significantly extended the lifespan of his e-MTB battery and enjoyed consistent performance for his daily commutes.

Final Thoughts

Understanding and managing the factors that influence the lifespan of an e-MTB battery is crucial for maintaining optimal performance and prolonging battery life. By practicing proper charging habits, monitoring usage patterns, and protecting the battery from extreme conditions, you can ensure that your e-MTB continues to provide reliable assistance for years to come. Implement these best practices, and you'll maximize your investment, making every ride more enjoyable and worry-free.

CHAPTER 33

Maximizing Your Battery's Lifespan

What are the best practices for charging and storing the battery to maximize its lifespan?

Ensuring the longevity and optimal performance of your electric assist mountain bike (e-MTB) battery hinges on adhering to correct charging and storage practices. Proper care not only extends the battery's lifespan but also ensures you get the most out of your rides. Let's explore the best practices for charging and storing your e-MTB battery in detail.

Best Practices for Charging Your e-MTB Battery

Avoid Deep Discharges

What to Do: Regularly charge your battery before it's completely drained. Ideally, recharge when it reaches around 20-30% capacity.

Why: Deep discharges can stress the battery, reducing its overall lifespan.

Example: Elise makes it a habit to charge her battery after rides, rarely letting it drop below 20%.

Do Not Overcharge

What to Do: Disconnect the charger once the battery is fully charged, typically when the indicator light on the charger turns green.

Why: Overcharging can cause overheating and degrade the battery chemistry.

Example: James sets a timer when charging his battery to remind him to unplug it as soon as it's fully charged.

Use the Manufacturer's Charger

What to Do: Always use the charger provided by or recommended by the battery manufacturer.

Why: Chargers are designed to match the battery specifications. Using a third-party charger can result in incorrect voltage, possibly damaging the battery.

Example: Laura ensures she only uses her Bosch charger for her e-MTB to maintain its integrity.

Charge at Moderate Temperatures

What to Do: Ensure the battery is at room temperature before charging.

Why: Charging a very cold or very hot battery can damage it.

Example: During winter, Joe brings his e-MTB battery indoors to warm up before charging.

Avoid Rapid Charging Excessively

What to Do: Use rapid charging sparingly and only when necessary.

Why: Frequent rapid charging can increase the battery's temperature, causing wear and tear.

Example: Samantha uses the standard charging setting, switching to rapid charge only when she needs a quick top-up.

Best Practices for Storing Your e-MTB Battery

Store at the Right State of Charge

What to Do: If you plan to store your e-MTB for more than a month, leave the battery charged to around 50-70%.

Why: Storing a fully charged or completely drained battery for long periods can stress it.

Example: Alex charges his battery to 60% before storing his e-MTB for winter.

Keep at Moderate Temperatures

What to Do: Store the battery in a cool, dry place, ideally between 10°C (50°F) and 25°C (77°F).

Why: Extreme temperatures, either hot or cold, can degrade the battery over time.

Example: Diane keeps her battery in a temperature-regulated basement when not in use.

Avoid Humidity and Moisture

What to Do: Store the battery in a dry environment, away from sources of moisture.

Why: Excessive humidity can lead to corrosion and damage the battery's electronics.

Example: Tom uses a dehumidifier in his storage area to maintain optimal conditions.

Regularly Inspect and Maintain

What to Do: Check the battery periodically during storage and recharge it if the voltage drops significantly.

Why: This helps maintain the battery's chemistry and prevents it from falling below a safe charge level.

Example: Carla inspects her stored battery every month and tops up the charge if necessary.

Use Protective Covers

What to Do: Consider using battery covers or cases during storage to protect against dust, dirt, and accidental damage.

Why: Keeping the battery clean and protected helps maintain its condition.

Example: Phil uses a padded case for his battery to prevent scratches and impacts.

Proper Storage Practices for Seasonal Riders

Mark rides his e-MTB extensively during the summer but stores it during the colder months. He follows best practices by charging his battery to 60% before storing it in his dry, climate-controlled basement. He places the battery in a padded case and checks it monthly, recharging slightly if necessary. By adhering to these practices, Mark ensures his battery remains in excellent condition, ready for the next riding season.

Final Thoughts

Adopting sound charging and storage habits for your e-MTB battery is essential for maximizing its lifespan and performance. By maintaining regular charging routines, storing the battery under optimal conditions, and following manufacturer recommendations, you can significantly extend the useful life of your battery. Implement these best practices, and you'll enjoy reliable performance on every ride, making the most of your investment in an electric assist mountain bike.

e-MTB Legal Regulations

What are the legal regulations regarding e-MTBs on trails?

Legal regulations concerning the use of electric assist mountain bikes (e-MTBs) on trails vary widely depending on geographic location, type of land, and local policies. Understanding these regulations is crucial to ensure that you ride responsibly, respect trail rules, and avoid potential fines or conflicts. Let's explore the legal landscape of e-MTBs, the factors influencing trail access, and best practices for compliance.

Understanding Legal Classifications

In many regions, e-MTBs are classified into different categories based on their motor power, speed capabilities, and the level of pedal assistance. Common classifications include:

Class 1 e-MTBs

Description: Equipped with a pedal-assist system that provides assistance only when the rider is pedaling and ceases to assist at speeds above 20 mph.

Trail Access: Generally allowed on most non-motorized trails alongside traditional mountain bikes.

Class 2 e-MTBs

Description: Include a throttle that can propel the bike without pedaling, with assistance also ceasing at 20 mph.

Trail Access: Access may be restricted on certain trails, especially those designated for non-motorized use only.

Class 3 e-MTBs

Description: Feature pedal-assist with no throttle, providing assistance up to 28 mph.

Trail Access: Typically restricted from non-motorized trails and allowed only on trails that permit motorized vehicles.

Federal and State Regulations (USA)

Federal Lands

National Parks: In the United States, the National Park Service (NPS) has allowed Class 1 e-MTBs on any trail where traditional mountain bikes are permitted, unless specifically prohibited by park management.

Bureau of Land Management (BLM): BLM policies may vary by region. Generally, Class 1 e-MTBs are the only class of e-bikes permitted on non-motorized trails.

State and Local Parks

Regulations may vary significantly from one state or municipality to another.

Example: California allows e-MTBs, including Class 1 and some Class 2, on most trails where traditional bikes are allowed. However, local jurisdictions may impose further restrictions.

International Regulations

European Union (EU)

Regulations: e-MTBs are generally classified as pedelecs, which provide pedal assistance up to 25 km/h (~15.5 mph) with a motor power limit of 250 watts.

Trail Access: Regulations can vary by country, but most EU countries allow pedelecs on trails where traditional mountain bikes are permitted.

Canada

Regulations: Vary by province. For instance, British Columbia allows Class 1 and Class 2 e-MTBs on multi-use trails, provided they fall within the provincial guidelines.

Trail Access: Some regions may permit e-MTBs on all trails open to mountain bikes, while others restrict their use to specific areas.

Factors Influencing Trail Access

Land Management Policies

Different types of land (federal, state, private) have varying rules regarding e-MTB access.

Example: Private landowners may set their own rules, so always check with local management or property owners.

Environmental Impact Studies

Concerns about trail erosion, wildlife disturbance, and user conflicts often influence regulatory decisions.

Example: Studies showing minimal impact by Class 1 e-MTBs compared to traditional bikes have led some areas to open non-motorized trails to e-MTBs.

User Conflicts

Perceived or actual conflicts between e-MTB riders and other trail users (hikers, equestrians) can lead to restrictions.

Example: Some trails designated for mountain biking may require additional signage or restrictions to manage multi-user dynamics.

Best Practices for Compliance

Research Local Regulations

Always check local rules before riding, as they can change frequently.

Resources: Use websites like Trailforks, MTB Project, and local land management sites for the most current information.

Engage with Local Communities

Join local e-MTB clubs and advocacy groups to stay informed about regulations and participate in discussions.

Example: Being part of groups like the Electric Mountain Bike Association (EMBA) can offer valuable insights and updates.

Follow Signage and Rules

Adhere to posted trail signs and respect areas marked as off-limits for e-MTBs.

Example: If a trailhead sign restricts motorized vehicles, ensure that your ride complies before proceeding.

Advocate Responsibly

Work with local advocacy groups to promote responsible e-MTB use and to educate other trail users about the benefits and regulations of e-MTBs.

Example: Collaborating with local land managers to plan designated e-MTB-friendly trails can foster positive community relations and expand access.

Navigating Regulations in Colorado

Lisa, a new e-MTB owner in Colorado, wanted to ride on local trails. She checked state regulations and found that Class 1 e-MTBs were generally allowed on non-motorized trails. Lisa joined her local mountain biking club and participated in their informational sessions to understand specific trail regulations better. This preparation ensured she rode in compliance with local rules, fostering a positive image of e-MTB users in her community.

Final Thoughts

Understanding and following the legal regulations regarding e-MTBs on trails is essential for responsible riding. By staying informed about your local, state, and federal regulations, adhering to best practices, and engaging with the community, you can enjoy the benefits of e-MTB riding while respecting trail access rules. This knowledge not only ensures a more harmonious trail-sharing environment but also helps to advocate for broader acceptance and access for e-MTBs in the future.

e-MTB Trail Access

Which trails are e-MTB friendly, and are there specific trail etiquette rules for e-MTB riders?

Finding e-MTB-friendly trails and understanding specific trail etiquette rules are fundamental for a safe and enjoyable riding experience. With the growing popularity of e-MTBs, many trails are now open for electric assist mountain bikers, but it's crucial to know where you can ride legally and how to conduct yourself appropriately on these trails.

Identifying e-MTB Friendly Trails

Here are some great resources to help you easily and reliably find e-MTB friendly trails.

Trailforks

How to Use: A popular trail database and mapping tool. Check the trail status and regulations section for e-MTB permissions.

Example: Searching for trails in Sedona, Arizona, Trailforks will indicate which trails are open to e-MTBs and provide user reviews for guidance.

MTB Project

How to Use: Another excellent online resource providing detailed descriptions and user feedback on trails. Look for e-MTB friendly tags and user comments regarding trail suitability.

Example: MTB Project lists trails in Moab, Utah, specifying those that allow e-MTBs and those restricted to non-motorized bikes.

Local Land Manager Websites

How to Use: Visit the websites of national parks, state parks, and local recreational areas. These sites often have the most up-to-date and accurate information on trail access rules for e-MTBs.

Example: The National Park Service (NPS) website offers specific guidelines for e-MTB use in parks like Acadia and Yosemite.

Local Bike Shops and Clubs

How to Use: Engage with the local mountain biking community through bike shops and clubs. They can provide firsthand information on which trails are e-MTB friendly.

Example: A local bike shop in Boulder, Colorado, recommended several e-MTB friendly trail systems, including Betasso Preserve and Marshall Mesa.

Example of e-MTB Friendly Trails

Whistler, British Columbia

The Whistler Valley Trail System allows e-MTBs on many of its multi-use trails, offering a mix of scenery and terrain.

Lake Tahoe, California/Nevada

Trails like the Tahoe Rim Trail and Flume Trail are open to Class 1 e-MTBs, providing stunning views and a challenging ride.

Park City, Utah

Known for its extensive trail network, Park City allows e-MTBs on several trails such as the Mid Mountain Trail and Armstrong Trail.

Specific Trail Etiquette Rules for e-MTB Riders

Respect Trail Access Rules

What to Do: Always verify if e-MTBs are allowed on a trail before riding. Adhere strictly to posted regulations.

Example: If a trail in Santa Cruz is marked as "non-motorized," do not ride your e-MTB there, even if traditional bikes are allowed.

Yield to Other Trail Users

What to Do: Follow the universal trail etiquette of yielding to hikers and equestrians. When encountering traditional mountain bikers, yield appropriately based on the trail's rules.

Example: On a shared trail in the Pisgah National Forest, slow down and announce your presence to hikers, yielding the right of way.

Manage Your Speed

What to Do: Maintain a safe speed, especially in crowded trail sections and when visibility is limited. Avoid excessive speeds downhill to prevent accidents.

Example: In bike parks like Whistler, adhere to speed limits in family-friendly areas and slow down when approaching blind corners. Announce your presence to avoid startling hikers or other mountain bikers that you may be passing, especially on uphill sections of trail where e-MTBs are much faster than manually powered bikes.

Be Aware of Battery Noise

What to Do: Be mindful that the motor noise may startle other trail users and wildlife. Approach slowly and announce your presence in advance.

Example: On the Cumberland Trail, gently announcing "rider approaching" helps avoid startling hikers with the e-MTB's motor noise.

Stay on Designated Trails

What to Do: Ride only on trails designated for e-MTBs to minimize erosion and environmental impact. Avoid creating new paths or cutting switchbacks.

Example: In Moab, stick to established e-MTB trails to help preserve the delicate desert ecosystem and reduce land degradation.

Join and Support Local Advocacy Groups

What to Do: Participate in or support local advocacy efforts to promote responsible e-MTB usage and trail access.

Example: Joining groups like the International Mountain Bicycling Association (IMBA) and participating in trail maintenance days helps foster positive relationships with land managers and other trail users.

Educate and Lead by Example

What to Do: Educate fellow e-MTB riders on best practices and proper etiquette to promote a positive image of e-MTB users.

Example: During group rides in areas like the Adirondacks, leading by example and following trail rules encourages others to do the same, enhancing the overall trail experience.

Enjoying e-MTB Trails in Oregon

Tom, an avid e-MTB rider, sought out e-MTB friendly trails in Oregon. Using Trailforks and connecting with a local bike shop, he identified trails like the Sandy Ridge Trail System and Oakridge. By following the trail rules and respecting other users, Tom enjoyed long, adventurous rides without any conflicts. In particular, he used a small bell so that other riders could hear him approaching when he rode on populated trails. This announced his presence without him having to remember to call out and at the same time prevented riders from being startled and potentially swerving off of the trail when he passed on uphill sections of trail where he typically was faster than riders without electric assist. He joined a local advocacy group to support trail maintenance and shared e-MTB etiquette tips with fellow riders, fostering a positive and respectful riding environment.

Final Thoughts

Finding e-MTB-friendly trails and adhering to specific trail etiquette rules is essential for a safe, enjoyable, and respectful riding experience. By using available resources, researching local regulations, and practicing responsible trail etiquette, you can explore a wide range of trails and contribute to a positive image of e-MTB riders. These practices ensure that e-MTBs are welcomed on more trails, enhancing the overall mountain biking community.

CHAPTER 36

Important Riding Techniques for e-MTB Riders

How do I manage the additional weight and power of an e-MTB on technical trails?

Managing the additional weight and power of an electric assist mountain bike (e-MTB) on technical trails requires a combination of technique, practice, and understanding of the bike's features. The motor and battery add significant weight, which affects handling, while the power assistance can change how you approach climbs and technical sections. Here are our best tips to help you master these aspects and ride confidently on technical trails.

Understanding the Impact of Additional Weight

Weight Distribution

Center of Gravity: The added weight from the motor and battery typically lowers the bike's center of gravity. This can enhance stability on straight sections but may require adjusted technique for handling sharp turns.

Example: On a technical descent in Whistler, Jason noticed his e-MTB felt more stable but required more effort to flick around tight switchbacks.

Momentum

Increased Momentum: The extra weight increases the bike's momentum. This can make it harder to stop quickly and more challenging to navigate tight spaces.

Example: When riding the technical trails in Moab, Emma had to start braking earlier and more gradually to maintain control.

Handling and Balance

Dual Suspension Setup: Many e-MTBs come with dual suspension, which helps manage the added weight. However, fine-tuning your suspension settings is crucial for optimal performance.

Example: Tom adjusted his suspension settings to a firmer setup when tackling technical rocky sections, allowing for better control and feedback.

Techniques for Managing Weight and Power

Cornering and Turns

Braking and Entry Speed: Approach corners with controlled braking. Enter turns at a steady speed to avoid the bike washing out.

Body Position: Lean your bike more than your body. Keep your weight centered over the bike and use your knees and elbows to absorb shocks.

Example: On the tight switchbacks of the Cumberland Trail, Sarah maintained a moderate speed and used controlled, gentle braking to navigate the turns smoothly.

Climbing Techniques

Seated Climbing: The weight of the e-MTB can make steep climbs more manageable when you stay seated. This maintains traction on the rear wheel.

Motor Assistance: Use the appropriate level of pedal assistance. Eco mode for less steep climbs to conserve battery, and higher modes for steeper inclines.

Example: During a climb in Marin County, Mark used the eco mode for gentle slopes and switched to a higher assistance level for the steeper sections, staying seated to maintain traction.

Descending Techniques

Weight Distribution: Shift your weight back to counteract the additional weight of the bike. Lower your center of gravity by bending your knees and elbows.

Controlled Speed: Use both brakes to modulate your speed, focusing slightly more on the rear brake to prevent skidding.

Example: On a technical descent in the Alpine Meadows, Alice shifted her weight back and kept her knees and elbows bent to absorb the shocks from rocks and roots.

Technical Obstacles

Rock Gardens and Root Sections: Keep your pedals level and use a steady cadence. Allow the bike to move beneath you while maintaining a relaxed grip on the handlebars.

Manual and Lift Technique: For obstacles like logs and large rocks, practice manualing (lifting the front wheel) to navigate smoothly.

Example: Navigating a rock garden on the Tahoe Rim Trail, Paul kept his pedals level and used a controlled, steady cadence to maintain balance and momentum.

Switchbacks and Tight Turns

Body Position: Approach switchbacks with your weight forward. Lean the bike into the turn while keeping your body upright.

Speed Management: Approach at a low speed and use controlled, gentle braking throughout the turn.

Example: On the technical switchbacks of Mount Tamalpais, Kelly approached each turn slowly, leaned her bike inward, and shifted her weight forward to stay balanced.

Optimizing Electric Assist

Adaptive Assistance

Modes: Most e-MTBs feature multiple assistance levels (eco, sport, turbo). Adapt the assistance level to the trail conditions to balance power and battery life.

Example: Simon used eco mode for flat sections and saved turbo mode for steep climbs and technical sections in the Scottish Highlands.

Smooth Transitions

Pedal Input: Provide consistent pedal input to avoid abrupt power surges. Smooth, steady pedaling is crucial for maintaining control.

Example: Fiona maintained a consistent pedal stroke while ascending a technical climb in the Lake District, ensuring smooth power delivery from her e-MTB.

Practice and Familiarity

Regular Practice

Spend time on various terrains to become familiar with how your e-MTB handles different conditions. Practice on both familiar and new trails to build confidence.

Example: Mark practiced regularly on local trails to get used to the additional weight and power of his e-MTB, improving his control and confidence over time.

Skill Clinics and Training

Consider attending skill clinics specifically designed for e-MTB riders. Professional trainers can provide valuable tips and techniques.

Example: Joining an e-MTB-specific skills clinic in Asheville helped Jane refine her riding techniques and learn how to handle her bike's power more effectively.

Mastering Technical Trails in Sedona

Laura, an intermediate mountain biker, struggled initially with the added weight and power of her new e-MTB. She practiced regularly on the technical trails of Sedona, focusing on key techniques like controlled braking, weight distribution, and consistent pedal input. Laura attended a local e-MTB clinic that provided hands-on training, enhancing her skills and confidence. Over time, she mastered the technical trails, enjoying the benefits of extended battery life and assisted climbs while navigating challenging terrain with ease.

Final Thoughts

Managing the additional weight and power of an e-MTB on technical trails requires a combination of specific techniques, practice, and familiarity with the bike's features. By focusing on proper body positioning, adaptive assistance, and consistent practice, you can ride confidently and efficiently on technical terrain. Embrace these strategies and enjoy the enhanced capabilities and extended adventures that your e-MTB offers.

CHAPTER 37

Tips for Riding eMTB's on Various Terrains

What specific handling techniques should I adopt for uphill and downhill riding with an e-MTB?

Uphill and downhill riding with an electric assist mountain bike (e-MTB) presents unique challenges and opportunities. Understanding and adopting specific handling techniques for both climbs and descents will help you make the most of your e-MTB, enhancing your performance, safety, and enjoyment. Here's what you need to know to mastering these techniques.

Uphill Riding Techniques

Consistent Pedaling for Motor Efficiency

Technique: Maintain a steady cadence and consistent pedal pressure. This helps the motor provide smooth assistance without sudden surges.

Example: Claire used a consistent pedaling rhythm on the steep climbs of Moab, ensuring her bike's motor delivered steady power without interruptions.

Seated Climbing for Traction

Technique: Stay seated during climbs to keep your weight over the rear wheel, enhancing traction. Lean slightly forward to keep the front wheel down.

Example: On the challenging climbs of the Colorado Trail, Mike remained seated to maintain rear wheel traction, preventing wheel spin on loose surfaces.

Adaptive Assistance Levels

Technique: Use lower assistance levels (eco mode) for gradual climbs to conserve battery and switch to higher levels (sport or turbo) for steeper, more demanding sections.

Example: Gregory alternated between eco and turbo modes while climbing in the Swiss Alps, optimizing battery use and maintaining steady progress.

Body Position Adjustment

Technique: Shift your weight forward slightly on steep climbs to keep the front wheel grounded. Lower your torso and keep elbows bent for better control.

Example: During a steep ascent in the Scottish Highlands, Emma leaned forward and lowered her upper body to keep her front wheel stable and improve control.

Downhill Riding Techniques

Controlled Speed Management

Technique: Use both brakes to maintain a controlled speed. Focus slightly more on the rear brake to avoid skidding and modulation issues.

Example: On the fast descents in the French Alps, Laura used controlled braking with a higher emphasis on the rear brake, maintaining stability and control.

Balanced Weight Distribution

Technique: Shift your weight back to maintain stability and control. Keep your knees and elbows bent to absorb shocks and maintain balance.

Example: While descending technical trails in Whistler, Jim shifted his weight back and kept his knees and elbows bent, enhancing control and absorbing impacts.

Line Choice and Pathfinding

Technique: Choose smooth, flowing lines that allow you to maintain momentum and minimize sudden braking or steering adjustments.

Example: On the rocky descents of the Flume Trail, Sarah focused on finding smooth lines that flowed naturally, reducing the need for abrupt corrections.

Body Position for Stability

Technique: Maintain a low center of gravity by bending your knees and elbows. Keep your body centered over the bike, allowing it to move freely beneath you.

Example: On the technical downhills of Pisgah National Forest, John kept a low center of gravity and allowed his bike to move under him, maintaining stability and control.

Handling Techniques for Mixed Terrain

Smooth Transitions Between Uphill and Downhill Riding

Technique: Anticipate changes in terrain and adjust body position, braking, and pedal assistance accordingly.

Example: During a mixed terrain ride in Lake Tahoe, Jessica smoothly transitioned from climbs to descents by adjusting her body position and motor assistance level ahead of time.

Consistent Pedal Input

Technique: Maintain consistent pedal input during transitions to prevent power surges and maintain control.

Example: On rolling hills in the Berkshires, Mark kept a steady pedal stroke, ensuring the motor delivered smooth power through varying terrain.

Proactive Braking and Steering

Technique: Use proactive braking and steering to navigate technical sections smoothly. Anticipate obstacles and adjust your line choice and brake usage in advance.

Example: Navigating technical sections in the Adirondacks, Rachel anticipated obstacles and used proactive braking and steering to maintain control and flow.

Mastering Mixed Terrain in the Rockies

David, an experienced e-MTB rider, frequently rides the varied terrains of the Rocky Mountains. He practices consistent pedaling, adaptive assistance levels, and precise body positioning to tackle steep climbs efficiently. On the descents, David focuses on controlled braking, balanced weight distribution, and smooth line choice to maintain stability. His approach ensures a seamless transition between different terrains, maximizing his riding performance and safety.

Final Thoughts

Adopting specific handling techniques for uphill and downhill riding with an e-MTB enhances your control, safety, and overall enjoyment. By focusing on consistent pedaling, adaptive assistance levels, and body positioning for climbs, and using controlled braking, balanced weight distribution, and proactive steering for descents, you can navigate technical trails with confidence. Regular practice and attention to these techniques will make you a more skilled and fulfilled e-MTB rider, ready to tackle any terrain.

eMTB Maintenance and Repair Basics

How do I maintain the electric components, such as the motor and battery, of my e-MTB?

Maintaining the electric components of your electric assist mountain bike (e-MTB) is crucial for ensuring optimal performance, longevity, and safety. The motor and battery are the core components that differentiate an e-MTB from a traditional mountain bike, and they require specific care. Here are the most important things you need to know to maintain these components effectively.

Motor Maintenance

Regular Inspection

Visual Check: Routinely inspect the motor for any visible signs of damage, dirt build-up, or loose connections. Look for cracks, dents, or corrosion.

Example: Lisa checks her mid-drive motor every week post-ride for any debris or damage, ensuring it's clean and secure.

Cleaning the Motor

Method: Use a soft, damp cloth to wipe the motor's exterior. Avoid using high-pressure water jets as water intrusion can damage internal components.

Example: Tom uses a microfiber cloth moistened with soapy water to gently clean his motor casing, avoiding electrical and moving parts.

Securing Connections

Check Connectors: Ensure that all electrical connectors and cables are properly attached and secured. Loose connections can lead to power loss and potential damage.

Example: Sarah regularly inspects the connections between her battery and motor, keeping them tight and secure to prevent any power interruptions.

Firmware Updates

Keep Software Updated: Some e-MTB motors require firmware updates for optimal performance. Check the manufacturer's website or contact your dealer for updates.

Example: John connects his e-MTB to the manufacturer's diagnostic tool once a year to ensure the motor firmware is up to date, enhancing efficiency and reliability.

Check for Overheating

Monitor Temperature: Overheating can degrade motor performance. If you notice excessive heat, give your bike a rest and avoid pushing the motor too hard.

Example: While on a long, steep climb, Alex stops occasionally to let his motor cool down, preventing overheating and preserving its functionality.

Battery Maintenance

Proper Charging Practices

Regular Charging: Charge your battery regularly, avoiding full discharges. It's best to recharge the battery when it drops to around 20-30%.

Avoid Overcharging: Disconnect the charger once the battery is fully charged to prevent overcharging.

Example: Maria sets an alarm to remind herself to unplug her battery once it's charged, maintaining its health and longevity.

Clean Battery Contacts

Method: Keep the battery contacts clean and free of dirt and corrosion. Use a dry cloth for regular cleaning and a contact cleaner if necessary.

Example: Chris uses a dry cloth to wipe down the battery terminals after each ride, ensuring good electrical connectivity.

Store at Optimal Charge and Temperature

Storage Charge: If storing the battery for an extended period, keep it charged to around 50-70%.

Temperature: Store the battery in a cool, dry place, ideally between 10°C (50°F) and 25°C (77°F).

Example: During winter, Emma stores her battery indoors at around 60% charge, keeping it in the basement where temperatures are stable.

Avoid Extreme Conditions

Temperature Tolerance: Avoid exposing the battery to extreme heat or cold. Both can negatively affect battery performance and lifespan.

Protection from Elements: Use protective covers if riding in wet or muddy conditions to shield the battery from moisture ingress.

Example: While riding in the rain, Gary covers his battery with a water-proof sleeve, preventing water damage.

Monitor Battery Health

Battery Management System (BMS): Many e-MTB batteries come with a built-in BMS that provides information on battery health. Regularly check status indicators.

Example: Laura uses the BMS app connected to her e-MTB to monitor battery health, ensuring it's performing optimally.

General Maintenance Tips

Regular Cleaning

Method: Clean your e-MTB after each ride, focusing on both electrical and mechanical components. Avoid high-pressure water near electric parts.

Example: After every muddy ride, Tom carefully cleans his bike with a gentle spray of water and a soft brush, paying extra attention to the motor and battery areas.

Professional Servicing

Frequency: Schedule professional servicing at least once a year to perform comprehensive checks and maintenance on both mechanical and electrical systems.

Example: Sarah takes her e-MTB to a certified service center annually, ensuring all components are checked and maintained, including motor diagnostics and battery health assessment.

DIY Basics

Knowledge: Equip yourself with basic knowledge of your e-MTB's components. Understanding how to perform simple checks and maintenance tasks can save time and money.

Example: Mike learned basic e-MTB maintenance from online tutorials, enabling him to confidently perform routine inspections and minor repairs.

Maintaining Longevity in the Rockies

Mark, an avid e-MTB rider, ensured the longevity and performance of his bike through diligent maintenance practices. He regularly cleaned his motor and battery, checked all connections, and adhered to proper charging routines. Mark also took his bike for annual professional servicing, where technicians updated firmware and performed thorough checks. His attention to detail not only kept his e-MTB functioning flawlessly but also extended the battery life and motor reliability, allowing him to enjoy countless adventures in the Rockies with peace of mind.

Final Thoughts

Maintaining the electric components of your e-MTB is essential for reliable performance and long-term durability. By following best practices for motor and battery care, including regular inspection, proper cleaning, optimized charging, and storage practices, you can ensure your e-MTB remains in top condition. This proactive approach to maintenance not only enhances your riding experience but also protects your investment, allowing you to enjoy the benefits of electric assist mountain biking for years to come.

<small>CHAPTER 39</small>

Troubleshooting Common e-MTB Issues

What are the common issues with e-MTBs, and how can I troubleshoot them?

Electric assist mountain bikes (e-MTBs) have complex systems that include mechanical and electrical components. While they are built to endure rigorous use, common issues can arise that affect performance. Being able to troubleshoot these problems can save you time and ensure a smooth riding experience. Here are the most important things for you to know about identifying and resolving common e-MTB issues.

Battery-Related Issues

Battery Not Charging

Common Causes: Faulty charger, damaged charging port, degraded battery cells.

Troubleshooting Steps:

Check Connections: Ensure all connections are secure. Inspect the charger and charging port for damage.

Test Charger: Use a multimeter to check if the charger is providing the correct output voltage.

Try a Different Outlet: Sometimes, the issue could be with the power outlet.

Example: Tom had a battery that wouldn't charge. He found that the charging port had accumulated dirt, which he cleaned carefully. The battery then charged without issue.

Battery Draining Quickly

Common Causes: Cold weather, old or degraded battery, high power consumption settings.

Troubleshooting Steps:

Check Battery Age: Batteries lose capacity over time. Consider if your battery is nearing the end of its lifespan.

Inspect for Cold Weather: Cold temperatures can reduce battery efficiency. Warm up the battery before use.

Optimize Power Settings: Use lower assistance modes to conserve battery life.

Example: During winter rides, Sarah noticed her battery drained quickly. She started warming up her battery indoors before riding, significantly extending battery life in cold conditions.

Motor-Related Issues

Motor Not Engaging

Common Causes: Loose connections, faulty sensors, firmware issues.

Troubleshooting Steps:

Secure Connections: Check all cables and connectors leading to the motor.

Sensor Check: Inspect torque and speed sensors for alignment and cleanliness.

Firmware Update: Ensure your motor firmware is up to date.

Example: Emma's motor wasn't engaging. Upon inspection, she found a loose connection at the motor's power cable, which she reconnected securely, resolving the issue.

Unusual Motor Noise

Common Causes: Debris in motor, worn bearings, loose components.

Troubleshooting Steps:

Clean Motor: Check for and remove any debris lodged in the motor casing.

Inspect Bearings: Listen for grinding noises indicating worn bearings.

Tighten Components: Ensure all mounting bolts and motor housing components are tight.

Example: Mark noticed a grinding noise from his motor. Upon inspection, he found a small rock lodged in the motor casing, which he removed, eliminating the noise.

Display and Control Issues

Display Not Turning On

Common Causes: Flat battery, faulty connections, defective display unit.

Troubleshooting Steps:

Battery Charge: Ensure the bike's battery is charged.

Check Connections: Inspect the connection between the display and the bike's electrical system.

Reset Display: Refer to the manufacturer's guide on resetting the display unit.

Example: Lisa's display wouldn't turn on. She found the connector had come loose during transport, and reattaching it fixed the problem.

Inaccurate Readings

Common Causes: Sensor misalignment, software glitches.

Troubleshooting Steps:

Realign Sensors: Ensure that speed and torque sensors are properly aligned and clean.

Software Update: Check for any available software updates for the display unit.

Example: Alex's speed readings were erratic. Realigning his speed sensor resolved the issue, providing accurate speed data.

General Mechanical Issues

Sudden Power Loss

Common Causes: Battery connection issues, overheating.

Troubleshooting Steps:

Check Connections: Ensure the battery is securely connected and the terminals are clean.

Overheating: Let the bike cool down and check if the issue persists.

Example: During a long ride, Emma experienced a power loss. She found that her battery had overheated. Allowing the bike to cool resolved the issue.

Drivetrain Problems

Common Causes: Chain wear, improper gear settings, and misaligned derailleur.

Troubleshooting Steps:

Inspect Chain: Check for chain wear and replace if necessary.

Gear Adjustment: Ensure the derailleur is properly aligned and gears shift smoothly.

Lubricate Drivetrain: Regularly lubricate the chain and drivetrain components.

Example: John's e-MTB had issues shifting gears. He realigned the derailleur and lubricated the chain, restoring smooth gear transitions.

Resolving Motor Engagement Issues on the Trail

During a group ride in the Rockies, Sarah's e-MTB motor suddenly stopped engaging. She quickly inspected the bike and found a loose connection at the motor's power cable. With a small multi-tool, she reconnected the cable securely, and the motor immediately began working again. This quick troubleshooting allowed her to continue the ride without significant delays.

Final Thoughts

Understanding and troubleshooting common e-MTB issues can greatly enhance your riding experience and prevent downtime. By regularly inspecting and maintaining your bike's electric components, and understanding how to address problems with the battery, motor, display, and drivetrain, you can keep your e-MTB in top condition. These proactive measures ensure that you can enjoy your rides to the fullest and respond effectively to any issues that arise.

CHAPTER 40

Maintaining and Repairing your e-MTB

Are there specific tools needed for e-MTB maintenance and repairs?

Maintaining and repairing an electric assist mountain bike (e-MTB) requires a mix of standard bike tools and a few specialized ones for dealing with the electric components. Having the right tools on hand makes routine maintenance and troubleshooting more efficient and effective. Here are the specific tools you'll need for e-MTB maintenance and repairs.

Standard Bike Maintenance Tools

Multi-Tool

Description: A compact tool that includes multiple Allen wrenches, screwdrivers, and sometimes a chain tool.

Use: Ideal for on-the-go adjustments, such as tightening bolts or adjusting derailleurs.

Example: The Topeak Alien II Multi-Tool is versatile and includes various tools needed for trail-side repairs.

Tire Levers

Description: Plastic or metal levers used to remove tires from the rim.

Use: Essential for fixing flats or replacing tires.

Example: Pedro's Tire Levers are durable and user-friendly.

Floor Pump with Gauge

Description: A pump with a built-in pressure gauge for inflating tires to the correct pressure.

Use: Maintaining proper tire pressure is crucial for performance and safety.

Example: The Lezyne Steel Floor Drive Pump offers precise pressure control.

Chain Tool

Description: A tool specifically designed to split and reconnect bike chains.

Use: Useful for chain repairs or replacement.

Example: The Park Tool CT-5 Mini Chain Brute is compact and easy to use.

Torque Wrench

Description: A wrench that measures the amount of torque applied to bolts.

Use: Ensures bolts are tightened to the manufacturer's specifications, preventing over-tightening.

Example: The VENZO Bicycle Torque Wrench offers precise torque measurements.

Hex and Torx Wrenches

Description: Sets of wrenches in various sizes, often needed for many bike components.

Use: Commonly used for assembling and adjusting components.

Example: The Park Tool AWS-1 Hex Wrench Set and TWS-1 Torx Wrench Set are high-quality options.

Screwdrivers

Description: Both flathead and Phillips screwdrivers.

Use: Used for adjusting components like derailleurs and securing accessories.

Example: Any reliable brand, such as Craftsman, will suffice.

Specialized Tools for e-MTB Maintenance

Battery Contact Cleaner

Description: A cleaner spray specifically designed for electrical contacts.

Use: Cleaning battery contacts and connectors to ensure good electrical conductivity.

Example: WD-40 Specialist Contact Cleaner is effective and safe for use on electronic components.

Digital Multimeter

Description: An electronic measuring instrument for checking voltage, current, and resistance.

Use: Diagnosing electrical issues, such as checking battery voltage or continuity in wires.

Example: The Fluke 115 Digital Multimeter is a reliable and accurate option.

Battery Tester

Description: A tool specifically designed to measure the health and state of charge of your e-MTB battery.

Use: Assessing battery performance and diagnosing battery-related issues.

Example: The Bosch BAT 218 Battery Tester is compatible with Bosch e-MTB batteries.

Cable Cutters

Description: Specialized cutters for bicycle cables and housing.

Use: Cutting and crimping new cables during replacement or adjustments.

Example: Park Tool CN-10 Professional Cable and Housing Cutters are designed for precision cuts.

Bottom Bracket Tool

Description: A tool used to remove and install the bottom bracket.

Use: Necessary for accessing and servicing mid-drive motors.

Example: The Park Tool BBT-9 Bottom Bracket Tool is compatible with many e-MTB models.

Freewheel Remover

Description: A tool for removing the bike's freewheel or cassette.

Use: Needed when replacing or servicing the rear wheel and motor assembly on hub-drive e-MTBs.

Example: The Park Tool FR-5.2G Cassette Lockring Tool is a versatile choice.

Spoke Wrench

Description: A small wrench designed to fit the spoke nipples on bicycle wheels.

Use: Truing wheels and maintaining spoke tension.

Example: The Park Tool SW-7.2 Triple Spoke Wrench fits most common spoke nipple sizes.

Other Useful Accessories

Work Stand

Description: A stand that holds the bike off the ground, allowing for easy access to all parts.

Use: Essential for performing detailed maintenance and repairs.

Example: The Park Tool PCS-10 Home Mechanic Repair Stand is sturdy and adjustable.

Degreaser and Lubricant

Description: Products used for cleaning and lubricating the chain and drivetrain components.

Use: Keeping the drivetrain clean and lubricated ensures smooth operation and longevity.

Example: The Finish Line Kit includes both degreaser and lubricant suitable for e-MTBs.

Protective Gloves

Description: Mechanic gloves protect your hands during maintenance and repairs.

Use: Preventing injuries and keeping your hands clean and safe.

Example: The Mechanix Wear Gloves are comfortable and durable for bike maintenance tasks.

Tackling a Mid-Ride Repair

During a remote trail ride, Mike experienced an unexpected chain break. Equipped with his multi-tool, chain tool, and spare master link, he quickly removed the damaged chain section and reconnected the chain, allowing him to continue his ride without significant delay. Having the right tools ensured that Mike could address the issue effectively, highlighting the importance of being prepared.

Final Thoughts

Having the right tools for maintaining and repairing your e-MTB is essential. By conducting routine maintenance and bringing a few tools with you on your rides you will get many miles (hours?) out of your bike, and save yourself unnecessary stress and inconvenience.

Please Tell Us What You Think

Dear Mountain Biking Enthusiast,

Thank you for choosing "Mastering Mountain Biking"! We've packed this book with everything you need to conquer trails and elevate your mountain biking experience.

Your journey with us doesn't end here. We'd love to hear how this book has impacted your rides and adventures. By sharing your thoughts, you'll not only help fellow bikers but also inspire more people to embrace the thrill of mountain biking.

Please take a moment to scan the QR code below or use the link and leave us a review. Your feedback is invaluable to us and to all eager riders looking to hit the trails with confidence.

https://amzn.to/4egi1E1

Happy trails and ride on!

Warm regards,

J. J. Quest

Thank You for Your Support

CHAPTER 41

Improving Your Fitness with an e-MTB

How can e-MTBs be used to improve fitness while reducing physical strain?

Electric assist mountain bikes (e-MTBs) are revolutionizing the way people approach fitness, making it easier and more enjoyable to get a good workout while reducing the physical strain associated with traditional mountain biking. By providing pedal assistance, e-MTBs allow riders to modulate their effort, making strenuous activities more accessible. Here's how e-MTBs can enhance your fitness routine while minimizing physical stress.

Adaptive Workouts

Tailored Intensity

Customization: e-MTBs allow you to adjust the level of assistance, enabling you to tailor the intensity of your workout to your fitness level and goals.

Example: Using a higher assistance level for challenging climbs allows a beginner to maintain a steady pace without overexertion, gradually building endurance.

Steady-State Rides

Consistent Effort: By utilizing the electric assist, riders can maintain a consistent effort level, avoiding the peaks and valleys of exertion typical in hilly or mountainous terrain.

Example: Karen uses her e-MTB's eco mode to maintain a consistent heart rate during her rides, gently easing up steep sections without spiking her effort.

Cardiovascular Benefits

Extended Riding Time

Longer Sessions: e-MTBs enable longer rides by reducing fatigue, thereby increasing cardiovascular endurance over time.

Example: Mark extends his rides from 30 minutes to over an hour using the assist features, significantly improving his cardiovascular fitness.

Interval Training

HIIT: Incorporate high-intensity interval training (HIIT) into your rides by switching between low and high assistance levels.

Example: Sarah alternates between low assistance on flat sections and high assistance on climbs, creating a HIIT workout that boosts her heart rate and burns calories efficiently.

Muscle Engagement

Balanced Muscle Use

Lower Body: The pedaling effort required to ride an e-MTB engages major muscle groups such as quadriceps, hamstrings, glutes, and calves.

Core Stability: Maintaining balance and control over varied terrains activates core muscles, enhancing stability and strength.

Example: Tim uses moderate assistance to tackle technical trails, engaging his entire lower body and core without overwhelming fatigue.

Reduced Impact

Joint Health: The assistance levels allow for reduced strain on joints, making it suitable for individuals with joint issues or recovering from injury.

Example: Emily, recovering from knee surgery, uses her e-MTB to rebuild strength and mobility without placing excessive stress on her healing joints.

Mental Health Benefits

Outdoor Activity

Exposure to Nature: Regular riding in natural settings can reduce stress, improve mood, and enhance mental well-being.

Example: Lisa finds solace in her daily e-MTB rides through forest trails, reporting reduced anxiety and improved mood.

Achievement and Progress

Goal Setting: Setting and achieving fitness goals with the help of an e-MTB boosts confidence and provides a sense of accomplishment.

Example: John sets weekly distance goals that he tracks, feeling a sense of achievement as he gradually improves his fitness.

Accessibility and Inclusivity

Inclusive Fitness

All Fitness Levels: e-MTBs make mountain biking accessible to a broader range of fitness levels, encouraging those who might be intimidated by traditional biking.

Example: Claire, a beginner, joins group rides using her e-MTB. The assist levels allow her to keep up with more experienced riders, enhancing her fitness in a supportive environment.

Adaptive Use

Physical Limitations: Individuals with physical limitations can use e-MTBs to engage in regular exercise, promoting cardiovascular fitness and muscle strength.

Example: David, who has a chronic illness, uses his e-MTB to stay active. The adjustable assistance allows him to control his exertion and avoid overexertion.

Practical Applications

Commuting

Active Transport: Using an e-MTB for commuting incorporates physical activity into daily routines without requiring a high level of exertion.

Example: Rachel commutes 10 miles each day on her e-MTB, enjoying the cardiovascular benefits and the beautiful scenery on her ride without arriving at work exhausted.

Recreational Riding

Adventurous Escapes: e-MTBs enable longer and more adventurous rides, keeping cycling enjoyable and engaging.

Example: Every weekend, Chris explores new trails with his e-MTB, combining fitness with the adventure of discovering new paths.

Improving Fitness with Recovery

Jessica, recovering from major knee surgery, found that riding up steep hills on her mountain bike was too hard on her knee, causing significant pain and swelling. By switching to an e-MTB, she was able to climb hills without overstressing her injured knee. Using moderate assistance, Jessica engaged in extended rides, improving her cardiovascular fitness and muscle strength without overstraining her joints. Her e-MTB became an integral part of her recovery process, allowing her to stay active and motivated.

Final Thoughts

e-MTBs offer a versatile and accessible way to improve fitness while reducing physical strain. By providing adjustable assistance, they enable riders to tailor their workouts, extend riding time, and engage multiple muscle groups effectively. The mental health benefits, inclusivity, and practical applications make e-MTBs an excellent choice for maintaining an active lifestyle. Embrace the advantages of electric assist mountain biking and enjoy the journey to improved fitness and well-being.

CHAPTER 42

Health Benefits with e-MTB's over Traditional Bikes

What are the health benefits of using an e-MTB compared to a traditional mountain bike?

Using an electric assist mountain bike (e-MTB) offers a range of health benefits that are comparable to, and in some cases enhanced over, those provided by traditional mountain bikes. The pedal assistance system enables riders to experience the physical and mental benefits of biking with reduced strain and fatigue. Riding an e-MTB is not "cheating"! Here are some of the top health benefits of using an e-MTB.

Cardiovascular Health

Improved Heart Health

Benefit: Riding an e-MTB can significantly improve cardiovascular health by promoting regular physical activity that strengthens the heart.

Example: Regular e-MTB rides have helped John lower his resting heart rate and blood pressure, reducing his risk of heart-related diseases.

Enhanced Endurance

Benefit: The assistance allows for longer riding sessions, gradually improving cardiovascular endurance over time without overwhelming fatigue.

Example: Maria's consistent e-MTB rides have increased her stamina, enabling her to enjoy longer distances and more challenging trails.

Muscle Strength and Tone

Engagement of Major Muscle Groups

Benefit: Pedaling an e-MTB engages the quadriceps, hamstrings, glutes, and calves while the core muscles stabilize the rider.

Example: After several months of e-MTB riding, Tom noticed improved muscle tone in his legs and a stronger core, enhancing his overall strength.

Balanced Workout

Benefit: The ability to modulate assistance allows riders to engage in balanced workouts, targeting different muscle groups effectively.

Example: Sarah alternates between high assistance on inclines and low assistance on flat sections, ensuring a comprehensive muscle workout.

Joint Health and Low Impact Exercise

Reduced Joint Strain

Benefit: The assistance provided by e-MTBs reduces strain on joints, making it a suitable exercise for individuals with joint issues or arthritis.

Example: Emily uses her e-MTB to remain active despite having knee arthritis, experiencing less pain and swelling compared to traditional biking.

Low Impact Exercise

Benefit: Cycling is a low-impact exercise that minimizes stress on the joints while providing effective cardiovascular and muscle benefits.

Example: David transitioned to an e-MTB after experiencing joint pain with running, finding it an excellent alternative that preserved his joint health.

Weight Management and Metabolic Health

Calorie Burning

Benefit: e-MTB rides can burn a considerable amount of calories, aiding in weight management and metabolic health.

Example: Lisa incorporated e-MTB rides into her weight loss regimen, successfully losing weight while enjoying outdoor adventures.

Improved Metabolic Rate

Benefit: Regular exercise on an e-MTB boosts metabolism, helping to regulate blood sugar levels and improve insulin sensitivity.

Example: Mark's consistent riding improved his metabolic rate and controlled his blood sugar levels, contributing to better overall health.

Mental Health Benefits

Reduced Stress and Anxiety

Benefit: Riding an e-MTB in natural settings reduces stress and anxiety, providing mental relaxation and clarity.

Example: Rachel finds that her anxiety levels decrease significantly after each e-MTB ride, contributing to better mental well-being.

Enhanced Mood

Benefit: Physical activity on an e-MTB stimulates the release of endorphins, enhancing mood and combating depression.

Example: Tim feels a noticeable boost in his mood and energy levels after his daily e-MTB rides, reporting better emotional health.

Accessibility and Encouragement of Regular Activity

Encouraging Consistent Exercise

Benefit: The ease of use and reduced physical strain encourage more frequent and consistent exercise, leading to sustained health benefits.

Example: Jessica, a beginner, found e-MTB riding less intimidating and more enjoyable, leading to a consistent exercise routine.

Inclusivity for Varying Fitness Levels

Benefit: e-MTBs make mountain biking accessible to individuals of varying fitness levels, promoting inclusivity and community engagement.

Example: Claire, initially hesitant due to her fitness level, joined community rides with her e-MTB, experiencing significant improvements in her health.

Practical Benefits for Daily Life

Integrative Commuting

Benefit: Using an e-MTB for commuting integrates physical activity into daily routines, promoting regular exercise without extra time commitments.

Example: Mike combines his daily 5-mile commute with exercise by using his e-MTB to ride to work. Riding stress free on trails and bike paths takes 7 minutes longer than he would spend stressed out, sitting in traffic in the car. Not only does he get a great workout and lowers his stress, but he saves himself an hour a day over driving and working out separately!

Rehabilitation and Recovery

Benefit: e-MTBs are useful for rehabilitation exercises, allowing gradual rebuilding of strength and mobility post-injury.

Example: After a shoulder injury, Alex used an e-MTB to regain strength and coordination without risking overexertion.

Health Transformation with e-MTB

Claire, a novice to mountain biking, was drawn to e-MTBs for their accessibility. Over the course of a year, Claire experienced significant health improvements. Her cardiovascular endurance improved, muscles became toned, and knee pain—which plagued her during other exercises—was no longer an issue. Additionally, her mental well-being flourished as she found a new passion in exploring trails and connecting with a supportive community. The versatility and reduced strain offered by her e-MTB transformed her fitness journey into a sustainable and enjoyable lifestyle.

Final Thoughts

Using an e-MTB provides numerous health benefits, from improved cardiovascular fitness and muscle strength to better mental health and joint preservation. These bikes encourage regular physical activity by making cycling accessible, enjoyable, and less strenuous. Whether you're looking to enhance your fitness routine, manage weight, or maintain joint health, e-MTBs offer a versatile and effective solution. Embrace the health benefits of electric assist mountain biking and discover a healthier, happier you.

CHAPTER 43

Cool Features Available on e-MTBs

What smart features are available on modern e-MTBs, and how can I use them effectively?

Modern electric assist mountain bikes (e-MTBs) come equipped with a range of smart features that enhance the riding experience, improve performance, and provide valuable data insights. Understanding these features and how to use them effectively can optimize your rides, ensure safety, and keep your e-MTB running smoothly. Here are some of the smart features commonly found on e-MTBs and how to make the most of them.

Integrated Displays

Description

Integrated displays, often mounted on the handlebars, provide real-time information such as speed, battery level, assistance mode, and range estimation.

Use

Speed Monitoring: Keep track of your speed to maintain a safe and controlled ride, especially on technical trails.

Battery Management: Monitor battery levels to plan your ride and avoid running out of power mid-trail.

Assistance Mode: Switch between different levels of pedal assistance (e.g., eco, tour, sport, turbo) based on terrain and effort needed.

Example

Emma, while riding in the Rockies, frequently checks her integrated display to monitor battery usage and adjust the assistance level, ensuring she can complete her planned route without depleting the battery.

GPS and Navigation Systems

Description

Many e-MTBs come with built-in GPS and navigation systems that help riders find and follow trails, track routes, and navigate back to starting points.

Use

Route Planning: Use GPS to plan your route and find the best trails suited to your skill level and preferences.

Trail Navigation: Follow real-time navigation prompts to stay on track and avoid getting lost, especially in unfamiliar areas.

Tracking Progress: Record your rides to review performance and share with the e-MTB community.

Example

Mark uses the GPS system on his e-MTB to navigate complex trail networks in Moab. The system helps him discover new trails and ensure he doesn't stray from his planned route.

Connectivity to Apps

Description

Modern e-MTBs can connect to various apps via Bluetooth or ANT+, offering advanced functionalities such as performance analysis, ride customization, and social sharing.

Use

Performance Analysis: Sync your e-MTB with apps like Strava or Garmin Connect to analyze your ride metrics, such as distance, elevation gain, and time.

Ride Customization: Use manufacturer-specific apps to customize motor assistance settings, update firmware, and calibrate sensors.

Community Engagement: Share your rides, follow fellow riders, and participate in challenges through connected apps to stay motivated and engaged.

Example

Lisa syncs her e-MTB with the Bosch eBike Connect app, allowing her to customize assistance modes and track detailed performance metrics, which she reviews post-ride to improve her fitness.

Anti-Theft Features

Description

Some e-MTBs are equipped with smart anti-theft systems, including GPS tracking, remote locking, and alarms.

Use

GPS Tracking: Monitor the location of your e-MTB in real time, providing peace of mind if your bike is left unattended.

Remote Locking: Lock your bike remotely via an app, disabling the motor to prevent unauthorized use.

Alarms: Receive instant notifications if your bike is tampered with or moved without authorization.

Example

While stopping for a break, David uses his e-MTB's app to activate the remote locking feature, ensuring his bike remains secure. He appreciates the peace of mind provided by the real-time GPS tracking.

Integrated Lights and Sensors

Description

Some e-MTBs come with integrated front and rear lights, as well as ambient light sensors that automatically adjust lighting based on conditions.

Use

Safety: Ensure visibility in low-light conditions or during nighttime rides with automated lights.

Convenience: Automatic light adjustment enhances safety and convenience, allowing you to focus on the ride.

Charge Management: Monitor the battery usage of lights to avoid reducing the main battery's longevity.

Example

Tom rides through varying light conditions and appreciates his e-MTB's automatic lights. They improve his visibility and safety without manual adjustments, especially during early morning rides.

Wireless Components

Description

Advanced e-MTBs may include wireless electronic shifting systems and dropper posts, providing seamless operation and reduced mechanical complexities.

Use

Electronic Shifting: Benefit from precise, reliable gear changes with electronic shifting systems like Shimano Di2 or SRAM Eagle AXS.

Wireless Dropper Posts: Simplify the use of dropper posts with wireless control, enhancing comfort and performance on technical trails.

Example

Sarah's e-MTB is fitted with SRAM Eagle AXS electronic shifting, providing her with smooth and effortless gear changes even on rough terrain.

Power Management and Range Extender

Description

Efficient power management systems and optional range extenders increase the usable range of your e-MTB, allowing for longer rides.

Use

Power Optimization: Use power management settings to optimize battery usage based on the terrain and ride type.

Range Extenders: Attach additional battery packs to extend your ride range, planning longer adventures without worrying about power.

Example

Emily uses a range extender on her e-MTB for multi-day bikepacking trips, ensuring she has sufficient power to cover extensive distances with confidence.

Leveraging Smart Features for Better Rides

Alex, an enthusiastic e-MTB rider, utilizes a variety of smart features to enhance his riding experience. He relies on the integrated GPS for navigation, especially when exploring new trails in the Alps. By syncing his e-MTB with the manufacturer's app, Alex customizes assistance settings to suit different terrains and reviews detailed ride metrics to track his progress. The anti-theft GPS tracking provides peace of mind when he leaves his bike unattended. These features collectively ensure Alex enjoys safe, efficient, and fulfilling rides, making the most of modern e-MTB technology.

Final Thoughts

Modern e-MTBs come with an array of smart features that can significantly enhance your riding experience. From integrated displays and navigation systems to connectivity with performance apps and advanced security measures, these technologies offer greater convenience, safety, and customization. By understanding and utilizing these features effectively, you can optimize your rides, monitor your performance, and ensure the longevity and security of your e-MTB. Embrace the smart capabilities of your e-MTB and elevate your mountain biking adventures to the next level.

CHAPTER 44

Integrating your e-MTB with Cycling Apps and other Digital Tools

How do I integrate my e-MTB with cycling apps and other digital tools for an enhanced riding experience?

Integrating your electric assist mountain bike (e-MTB) with cycling apps and digital tools can significantly enhance your riding experience, providing detailed performance metrics, route planning, social interaction, and more. Understanding how to connect your e-MTB to these technologies and leverage their capabilities will help you make the most of your rides. Here's what you need to know about integrating your e-MTB with cycling apps and digital tools.

Understanding Connectivity Options

Bluetooth and ANT+ Integration

Description: Most modern e-MTBs are equipped with Bluetooth and/or ANT+ connectivity, allowing them to sync with various cycling apps and devices.

Example: Lisa's e-MTB uses Bluetooth to connect seamlessly with her smartphone, enabling integration with multiple apps.

Setting Up and Syncing with Cycling Apps

Strava

Features: Track your rides, analyze performance, follow other riders, and participate in challenges.

How to Use:

Connect Your e-MTB: Ensure your e-MTB's Bluetooth is activated, then open the Strava app and navigate to the device settings to connect.

Track and Analyze Rides: Once connected, start a ride to record metrics such as distance, speed, elevation, and heart rate (if using a heart rate monitor).

Example. Emma uses Strava to track her mountain biking routes in the Rockies, comparing her performance over time and setting new personal records.

Garmin Connect

Features: Detailed performance analysis, custom training plans, and route planning.

How to Use:

Sync with Garmin Device: Connect your e-MTB to a Garmin bike computer or smartwatch via Bluetooth or ANT+, then sync the device with the Garmin Connect app.

Plan Routes and Analyze Data: Use Garmin Connect to plan routes, navigate trails, and review detailed ride metrics.

Example: Tom uses his Garmin Edge bike computer to monitor his ride metrics in real-time, then syncs with Garmin Connect to analyze his performance and plan future routes.

Bosch eBike Connect

Features: Customization of assistance levels, firmware updates, ride data analysis, and navigation.

How to Use:

Connect to Bosch System: Ensure your Bosch e-MTB system is connected via Bluetooth to the eBike Connect app.

Customize Settings and Track Rides: Use the app to adjust motor assistance settings, update firmware, and track ride data.

Example: Mark uses the Bosch eBike Connect app to customize his e-MTB's assistance modes for different terrains, and monitor his battery usage during long rides.

Komoot

Features: Route planning with turn-by-turn navigation, offline maps, and community recommendations.

How to Use:

Sync with e-MTB: Connect Komoot to your e-MTB's display or bike computer via Bluetooth.

Plan and Follow Routes: Use Komoot to plan detailed routes and receive turn-by-turn navigation prompts during rides.

Example: Sarah plans her weekend rides using Komoot, discovering new trails and receiving navigation assistance directly on her e-MTB's display.

Trailforks

Features: Comprehensive trail database, user reviews, GPS navigation, and trail conditions.

How to Use:

Connect to Device: Sync Trailforks with your e-MTB's GPS-enabled display or your smartphone.

Explore Trails: Find and navigate trails, check trail conditions, and contribute reviews and photos.

Example: David uses Trailforks to explore new trails in Moab, checking trail conditions and navigating difficult sections with the app's GPS features.

Enhancing Your Riding Experience with Digital Tools

Performance Sensors

Heart Rate Monitors. Connect a Bluetooth or ANT+ heart rate monitor to your e-MTB or cycling app to track your cardiovascular performance.

Power Meters: Measure your power output in watts, providing insights into your pedaling efficiency and strength.

Example: John uses a heart rate monitor synced to his GPS bike computer, analyzing his cardiovascular performance during each ride.

Wearable Devices

Smartwatches: Devices like the Garmin Forerunner or Apple Watch offer performance tracking, navigation, and health monitoring.

Example: Emily uses her Garmin Forerunner to track her rides and monitor her heart rate, receiving real-time updates and post-ride analysis.

Social Sharing and Challenges

Joining Challenges: Participate in community challenges on apps like Strava to stay motivated and engage with other riders.

Social Integration: Share your rides and achievements on social media platforms, connecting with a broader cycling community.

Example: Lisa regularly participates in monthly distance challenges on Strava, sharing her progress with friends and fellow riders.

Firmware Updates and Customization

Regular Firmware Checks: Ensure your e-MTB firmware is up to date to maintain optimal performance and access new features.

Custom Assistance Settings: Use manufacturer apps to customize motor assistance levels to suit different terrains and riding styles.

Example: Mike updates his e-MTB's firmware through the Bosch eBike Connect app, benefiting from improved performance and new customization options.

Integrated Technology for Seamless Rides

Jessica, an avid e-MTB rider, effectively uses digital tools to enhance her riding experience. She connects her e-MTB to Strava for performance tracking, uses Komoot for detailed route planning and navigation, and syncs her rides with Garmin Connect for post-ride analysis. Jessica wears a Garmin smartwatch to monitor her heart rate and track her fitness progress. By leveraging these connected technologies, Jessica enjoys informed, safer, and more engaging rides, continuously improving her fitness and discovering new trails.

Final Thoughts

Integrating your e-MTB with cycling apps and digital tools can significantly enhance your riding experience. By connecting to performance tracking apps, utilizing GPS navigation, and engaging with social platforms, you can optimize your rides, improve your fitness, and connect with a supportive community. Embrace the functionalities offered by modern e-MTB technologies and make the most of your mountain biking adventures.

CHAPTER 45

Contributing to Sustainability

How do e-MTBs contribute to sustainable transportation and recreation?

Electric assist mountain bikes (e-MTBs) have emerged as a sustainable mode of transportation and recreation, offering numerous environmental and practical benefits. By reducing reliance on fossil fuels, promoting outdoor activity, and encouraging eco-friendly practices, e-MTBs play a significant role in sustainability. Here's how e-MTBs contribute to sustainable transportation and recreation.

Reduced Carbon Footprint

Lower Emissions

Benefit: e-MTBs produce zero direct emissions, reducing the overall carbon footprint associated with transportation.

Example: Emma uses her e-MTB for daily commutes instead of driving, significantly cutting down her carbon emissions and contributing to cleaner air.

Energy Efficiency

Benefit: e-MTBs are highly energy-efficient compared to motor vehicles, requiring far less energy to operate.

Example: Mark's e-MTB consumes minimal electricity, particularly when charged using renewable energy sources like solar power, enhancing his sustainable transportation efforts.

Sustainable Recreation

Eco-Friendly Exploration

Benefit: e-MTBs allow riders to explore natural landscapes with minimal environmental impact, promoting eco-friendly recreation.

Example: Lisa enjoys scenic rides through national parks on her e-MTB without contributing to noise and air pollution, leaving nature undisturbed.

Trail Preservation

Benefit: When ridden responsibly, e-MTBs minimize trail erosion and environmental disruption compared to heavier motorized vehicles.

Example: Sarah follows trail etiquette guidelines, riding only on designated paths and avoiding sensitive areas, preserving the natural beauty of the trails.

Promoting Active Transportation

Health and Sustainability

Benefit: e-MTBs encourage a more active lifestyle, reducing reliance on cars and fostering better physical health.

Example: Michael combines his fitness routine with sustainable transportation by using his e-MTB for both commuting and recreational purposes.

Last-Mile Connectivity

Benefit: e-MTBs provide efficient solutions for last-mile connectivity, bridging the gap between public transportation hubs and final destinations.

Example: Rachel uses her e-MTB to travel from the train station to her workplace, eliminating the need for a car and promoting a seamless, eco-friendly commute.

Encouraging Eco-Tourism

Sustainable Travel

Benefit: e-MTBs facilitate eco-tourism by enabling travelers to explore environmentally sensitive areas without causing harm.

Example: Jason embarks on e-MTB guided tours of protected landscapes, enjoying nature while supporting local conservation efforts.

Community Engagement

Benefit: e-MTB eco-tourism initiatives can promote community involvement in conservation and sustainable practices.

Example: Local tour operators in the Swiss Alps provide e-MTB rentals and guided eco-tours, educating riders on sustainable travel practices and supporting community-based conservation programs.

Resource Efficiency

Energy and Material Savings

Benefit: The manufacturing processes and operational energy requirements for e-MTBs are considerably lower than those for cars and motorcycles.

Example: Claire's investment in an e-MTB reduces her overall consumption of resources, contributing to a more sustainable lifestyle.

Batteries and Renewable Energy

Benefit: As battery technology improves and renewable energy sources become more prevalent, the environmental impact of charging e-MTBs continues to decrease.

Example: Alex charges his e-MTB using solar panels, further reducing his reliance on non-renewable energy and enhancing sustainability.

Long-Term Environmental Impact

Longevity and Durability

Benefit: High-quality e-MTBs are designed for longevity and durability, reducing the need for frequent replacements and minimizing waste.

Example: David invests in a durable e-MTB with a high lifespan, ensuring he can enjoy sustainable rides for many years without contributing to electronic waste.

Recycle and Reuse Programs

Benefit: Many manufacturers offer battery recycling programs and encourage the repurposing of components, promoting circular economy practices.

Example: Susan participates in her e-MTB manufacturer's battery recycling initiative, ensuring her old battery is responsibly recycled.

Policy and Advocacy Support

Advocacy for Sustainable Infrastructure

Benefit: e-MTBs promote the development of biking infrastructure, including bike lanes and charging stations, supporting broader sustainability goals.

Example: Tom advocates for the expansion of bike lanes and e-MTB charging stations in his city, encouraging the adoption of sustainable transportation.

Support for Environmental Policies

Benefit: e-MTBs align with and support environmental policies aimed at reducing carbon emissions and promoting sustainable transportation.

Example: Local governments in California provide incentives for e-MTB purchases, aligning with state policies to reduce greenhouse gas emissions.

Sustainable Commuting and Recreation

Jessica, an environmental enthusiast, integrates sustainability into her lifestyle by using her e-MTB for both commuting and recreational purposes. She charges her e-MTB using solar energy, actively participates in trail maintenance programs, and supports local eco-tourism initiatives. Jessica's commitment to sustainability not only reduces her carbon footprint but also promotes environmental conservation, inspiring others in her community to adopt eco-friendly practices.

Final Thoughts

E-MTBs contribute significantly to sustainable transportation and recreation by reducing carbon emissions, promoting active and eco-friendly lifestyles, and supporting environmental conservation efforts. By embracing e-MTBs, riders can enjoy the benefits of outdoor exploration, improved health, and reduced environmental impact. The integration of e-MTBs into daily life and recreational activities supports broader sustainability goals, fostering a greener and more responsible future.

CHAPTER 46

Environmental Considerations When Riding eMTBs

What environmental considerations should I keep in mind when using an e-MTB?

While electric assist mountain bikes (e-MTBs) offer numerous environmental benefits, it's essential to ride responsibly and be mindful of the impact of riding on natural landscapes and ecosystems. Understanding and applying environmental considerations ensures that your e-MTB use aligns with sustainable practices and minimizes ecological disruption. Here are some of the environmental considerations you should keep in mind when using an e-MTB.

Responsible Trail Use

Stay on Designated Trails

Importance: Riding on designated trails prevents damage to vegetation and minimizes soil erosion, preserving the natural environment.

Example: Sarah always follows trail markers and stays on official paths, avoiding off-trail riding that could harm fragile ecosystems.

Avoid Sensitive Areas

Importance: Refrain from riding through sensitive habitats, such as wetlands, wildlife habitats, and areas prone to erosion.

Example: Alex carefully navigates around sensitive areas in national parks, respecting signage and guidelines to protect delicate ecosystems.

Respect Seasonal Closures

Importance: Some trails may be seasonally closed to protect wildlife during breeding periods or to prevent trail damage in wet conditions.

Example: During spring, Emma avoids trails marked for seasonal closure to protect nesting birds and allow trail recovery.

Sustainable Riding Practices

Minimize Impact on Trails

Technique: Use appropriate tire pressure and suspension settings to reduce trail wear and prevent excessive erosion.

Example: Mark adjusts his tire pressure and suspension settings based on trail conditions, ensuring his e-MTB ride leaves minimal impact.

Ride Smoothly and Predictably

Technique: Avoid sudden braking and sharp turns that can cause trail damage and increase erosion.

Example: Lisa rides at a consistent pace, using smooth braking and turning techniques to preserve trail integrity.

Leave No Trace

Principle: Follow the Leave No Trace principles by packing out all trash, not disturbing wildlife, and leaving natural resources undisturbed.

Example: Claire carries a small trash bag on her rides, ensuring she leaves natural areas as pristine as she found them.

Battery Management

Efficient Charging Practices

Importance: Charge your e-MTB battery using renewable energy sources whenever possible, such as solar panels or green energy providers.

Example: David charges his e-MTB using a home solar panel setup, reducing his reliance on fossil fuels and minimizing environmental impact.

Battery Disposal and Recycling

Principle: Properly recycle or dispose of e-MTB batteries at designated disposal centers to prevent hazardous waste and environmental contamination.

Example: Jessica participates in her local bike shop's battery recycling program, ensuring her old battery is disposed of responsibly.

Battery Life Maximization

Technique: Follow best practices for charging and storage to extend battery lifespan, reducing the frequency of replacements.

Example: Tom maintains his battery by keeping it charged to optimal levels and storing it in a cool, dry place during off-seasons.

Wildlife and Ecosystem Respect

Avoid Wildlife Disturbance

Principle: Respect wildlife by giving animals plenty of space, avoiding loud noises, and not feeding or approaching them.

Example: Emma quietly observes wildlife from a distance while riding through forested trails, ensuring she does not disturb their natural behavior.

Stay Informed About Local Ecosystems

Education: Learn about the ecosystems of the areas you ride in to understand the potential impacts and how to mitigate them.

Example: Mark attends local conservation workshops to learn about the unique flora and fauna of the trails he frequents, enhancing his respectful riding practices.

Trail Maintenance and Advocacy

Participate in Trail Maintenance

Involvement: Join local trail maintenance groups to help preserve and improve trail conditions, ensuring sustainable use for all.

Example: Alex volunteers for monthly trail maintenance events, contributing to the upkeep and sustainability of his favorite riding spots.

Support Advocacy Efforts

Contribution: Support organizations that advocate for sustainable trail usage, conservation, and e-MTB access.

Example: Lisa donates to the International Mountain Bicycling Association (IMBA), supporting their efforts to promote sustainable biking practices.

Eco-Friendly Gear and Accessories

Choose Sustainable Products

Principle: Opt for biking gear and accessories that are environmentally friendly, such as products made from recycled materials.

Example: Claire selects bike bags and clothing made from sustainable materials, supporting eco-friendly companies.

Reuse and Recycle Gear

Practice: Extend the life of your biking gear by repairing rather than replacing, and recycle items that are no longer usable.

Example: Emma repairs her biking gloves and helmet straps instead of buying new ones, reducing waste and supporting sustainability.

Practicing Sustainable Riding in National Parks

Rachel, an environmentally conscious rider, follows best practices to minimize her impact on natural trails. She always stays on designated paths, participates in local trail maintenance, and charges her e-MTB using solar energy. Additionally, Rachel educates herself about local wildlife and ecosystems, ensuring her rides are respectful and sustainable. Her commitment to environmental considerations ensures that she enjoys nature while preserving it for future generations.

Final Thoughts

Riding an e-MTB responsibly and sustainably involves a combination of mindful practices, respect for nature, and active participation in conservation efforts. By staying on designated trails, managing battery life efficiently, respecting wildlife, and supporting trail maintenance and advocacy, you can minimize your environmental impact. Embrace these sustainable practices to ensure that your e-MTB adventures contribute positively to the preservation of natural landscapes and ecosystems.

CHAPTER 47

Connecting with Other e-MTB Riders

How do I connect with other e-MTB riders and clubs?

Connecting with other e-MTB riders and joining local clubs is an excellent way to enhance your riding experience, improve your skills, and foster a sense of community. Shared experiences, group rides, and club events can provide invaluable support and motivation. Here are some ideas for how to connect with fellow e-MTB enthusiasts and join clubs.

Online Platforms and Social Media

Meetup

How to Use: Visit Meetup.com and search for e-MTB or mountain biking groups in your area. Join the groups that interest you and participate in their events.

Example: Lisa found an e-MTB group in her city on Meetup, joined their regular weekend rides, and made new riding friends.

Facebook Groups

How to Use: Use Facebook's search function to find local and global e-MTB groups. Join these groups, introduce yourself, and engage in discussions.

Example: Mark joined the "Electric Mountain Bikers USA" group on Facebook, where he shares his rides and gets tips from other members.

Reddit

How to Use: Join subreddits dedicated to mountain biking, such as r/MTB or r/mountainbiking. Look for threads or create posts asking about e-MTB groups in your area.

Example: Sarah posted on r/mountainbiking looking for e-MTB groups in Oregon and received several recommendations for local clubs and events.

Local Bike Shops and Riding Centers

Ask for Recommendations

How to Use: Visit local bike shops and ask the staff about e-MTB clubs or group rides. They often have information about local communities and can provide insider tips.

Example: Tom's local bike shop recommended a popular e-MTB club in his town, where he now participates in weekly rides.

Bulletin Boards

How to Use: Many bike shops have bulletin boards or flyers advertising local rides and events. Check these regularly for updates on group rides and meetings.

Example: Emma found a flyer for a monthly e-MTB meetup at her local trail center and decided to join, connecting with fellow enthusiasts.

Trail Organizations and Events

Local Trail Organizations

How to Use: Research local trail organizations or biking associations and join them. These groups often organize rides, maintenance days, and other events.

Example: David joined his local chapter of the International Mountain Bicycling Association (IMBA) and participates in their organized rides and trail work days.

Bike Parks and Trailheads

How to Use: Visit bike parks and popular trailheads, where riders often gather. Engage with other riders to learn about local clubs and upcoming rides.

Example: Claire struck up a conversation with a group of riders at her local bike park and was invited to join their riding club.

Formal Clubs and Associations

IMBA (International Mountain Bicycling Association)

How to Use: Visit the IMBA website to find local chapters near you. Join a chapter to get involved in group rides, trail building activities, and advocacy efforts.

Example: Lisa joined her local IMBA chapter, where she participated in group rides and became active in trail maintenance projects.

Regional Clubs and Associations

How to Use: Look for regional biking clubs and associations dedicated to mountain biking and e-MTBs.

Example: Mark joined "NorCal E-MTB Riders," a regional club offering organized rides, skills clinics, and social events.

Group Rides and Clinics

Group Rides

How to Use: Join local group rides organized by clubs, bike shops, or online communities. These rides offer opportunities to meet other e-MTB enthusiasts.

Example: Sarah regularly joins group rides organized by her local bike shop, expanding her network of friends and fellow riders.

Skills Clinics

How to Use: Attend mountain biking skills clinics offered by local bike shops, trail organizations, or clubs. These clinics often attract riders of similar skill levels.

Example: Tom attended an e-MTB skills clinic, where he improved his riding techniques and connected with other participants.

Advocacy and Volunteer Efforts

Trail Maintenance

How to Use: Volunteer for trail maintenance and building projects organized by local trail organizations or biking clubs.

Example: David volunteered for a trail maintenance day organized by his local IMBA chapter, where he met other passionate riders and contributed to the community.

Advocacy Events

How to Use: Participate in advocacy events and campaigns to promote e-MTB access and sustainable trail use. This can be especially important as various organizations are deciding whether to lump class 1 pedal assist e-MTBs in with the same rules that apply to fully motorized dirt bikes.

Example: Emma attended a local advocacy meeting to discuss e-MTB trail access, connecting with community leaders and fellow riders. Due to the large number of e-MTB attendees, the community leaders voted to allow Class 1 e-MTBs on trails reserved for classical mountain bikes.

Competitive and Recreational Events

Local and Regional Races

How to Use: Participate in local and regional e-MTB races or fun rides to meet other competitive and recreational riders.

Example: Claire entered a regional e-MTB race and connected with other racers, forming new friendships and sharing experiences.

Recreational Events

How to Use: Attend recreational biking events, such as festivals and demo days, which often include opportunities to test new bikes and gear.

Example: While attending a biking festival, Tom participated in demo rides and met other e-MTB enthusiasts, expanding his riding network.

Building Community Through Group Rides

Jessica, an avid e-MTB rider, was eager to connect with other riders in her area. She joined a local e-MTB group on Facebook and started participating in their weekly rides. Through these group rides, Jessica made new friends, learned about local trails, and even participated in trail maintenance days. She also attended skills clinics and advocacy events, further deepening her involvement in the e-MTB community. Jessica's proactive approach helped her build a supportive network of fellow riders and enabled her to learn about new trails to ride, enhancing her overall riding experience.

Final Thoughts

Connecting with other e-MTB riders and clubs enriches your mountain biking experience by providing support, shared knowledge, and a sense of community. By leveraging online platforms, local bike shops, trail organizations, and participating in group rides and events, you can build a network of enthusiastic riders. Embrace these opportunities to connect, learn, and contribute to the growing community of e-MTB enthusiasts.

CHAPTER 48

Events and Races for e-MTBs

What are some popular mountain biking events or races I can participate in with an e-MTB?

Participating in mountain biking events and races specifically catering to e-MTB riders is an excellent way to challenge yourself, meet fellow e-MTB enthusiasts, and immerse yourself in the dedicated community. Here are some of the top events and races where e-MTB riders are welcome on their electric bikes.

Specialized eMTB Series (2024)

Specialized eMTBSeries

Description: This exciting series features multiple events across different locations, specifically designed for e-MTB riders.

Why Participate: This series offers a unique blend of technical challenges, endurance rides, and fun social elements, all while promoting the capabilities and benefits of e-MTBs.

Example: Emma joined the Specialized eMTB Series event in her region, tackling diverse trails and engaging with like-minded riders, enhancing her riding skills and enjoying the community spirit.

Enduro World Series (EWS-E)

EWS-E Races

Description: The Enduro World Series has added e-MTB categories across various global locations, blending enduro racing with the unique aspects of e-MTB riding.

Why Participate: Compete at an international level and experience stages designed to test both technical skills and battery management.

Example: Mark competed in the EWS-E race in Italy, experiencing challenging terrains while strategically managing his e-MTB's assistance levels.

UCI e-Mountain Bike Cross-Country World Cup

UCI e-MTB World Cup

Description: This prestigious event features top-level competition for e-MTB riders worldwide, pitting them against each other on demanding cross-country courses.

Why Participate: Compete against the best, experience top-tier race organization, and gain international exposure.

Example: Lisa participated in the UCI e-MTB event in Switzerland, relishing the opportunity to race against world-class competitors and pushing her limits.

Sea Otter Classic (e-MTB Category)

Sea Otter Classic e-MTB

Description: This well-known cycling festival includes races for e-MTB riders, alongside its vast array of biking events and expos.

Why Participate: Enjoy the festival atmosphere, explore the latest biking gear, and race on challenging courses designed for e-MTBs.

Example: David raced in the e-MTB category at the Sea Otter Classic, enjoying the competitive spirit and the festival's vibrant community.

Roc d'Azur (e-MTB Events)

Roc d'Azur e-MTB

Description: One of the largest mountain biking festivals in the world, the Roc d'Azur now features events specifically for e-MTB riders.

Why Participate: Compete in a range of e-MTB races while experiencing the festival atmosphere and community.

Example: Sarah participated in the Roc d'Azur e-MTB events, enjoying the vast array of races and the chance to meet international e-MTB enthusiasts.

Crankworx (e-MTB Category)

Crankworx e-MTB

Description: The Crankworx festival includes specialized e-MTB events, combining downhill, slopestyle, and enduro elements.

Why Participate: Participate in diverse and thrilling competitions and enjoy the festival's celebrations and camaraderie.

Example: Tom competed in the e-MTB category at Crankworx Whistler, experiencing the excitement of downhill racing and the supportive community spirit.

Big Mountain Enduro (e-MTB Category)

Big Mountain Enduro e-MTB

Description: This popular enduro race series includes categories for e-MTB riders, featuring rugged mountainous terrains and technical challenges.

Why Participate: Test your skills on some of North America's toughest terrains and enjoy the company of fellow endurance racers.

Example: Emma eagerly took on the Big Mountain Enduro race in Colorado, relishing the technical courses and the opportunity to connect with other e-MTB enthusiasts.

Swiss Epic (e-MTB Category)

Swiss Epic e-MTB

Description: Known for its stunning alpine scenery and challenging stages, the Swiss Epic includes a category for e-MTB riders.

Why Participate: Enjoy multi-day racing through Switzerland's iconic landscapes with comprehensive event support and camaraderie.

Example: Lisa joined the e-MTB category in the Swiss Epic, navigating breathtaking trails while managing her bike's battery to last through the stages.

Australian e-Mountain Bike National Championships

Australian e-MTB Nationals

Description: This event specifically caters to e-MTB riders, offering competitive racing opportunities in various categories.

Why Participate: Compete at a national level and experience unique Australian trails.

Example: David raced in the Australian eMTB Nationals, enjoying the spirited competition and diverse terrains Down Under.

TransRockies eMTB

TransRockies eMTB

Description: A multi-day stage race through the Canadian Rockies, featuring an e-MTB category with stunning backdrops and rigorous trails.

Why Participate: Challenge yourself in a spectacular setting with well-organized support and logistics.

Example: Sarah tackled the TransRockies eMTB race, experiencing the rugged beauty of the Rockies while competing in an endurance challenge.

Jessica's Journey into e-MTB Racing

As a competitive tri-athlete, Jessica had always been passionate about mountain biking but found herself increasingly drawn to the unique capabilities and community of e-Mountain Biking (e-MTB) after she injured her knee skiing and was unable to climb steep hills without pedal assist. After purchasing her first top-of-the-line e-MTB, she was eager to explore not just the trails around her hometown but also the competitive world of e-MTB racing.

Curious about where to start, Jessica decided to join one of the most prominent events tailored for e-MTB riders: the Specialized eMTB Series. The event promised a mix of technical challenges, social rides, and a vibrant community of like-minded riders. She selected an event happening in a picturesque region known for its diverse trails and signed up with a mix of excitement and nerves.

Upon arrival, Jessica was immediately struck by the energetic atmosphere. She attended a pre-race briefing, met fellow competitors, and received tips from seasoned racers. The event included a variety of stages, each designed to test different aspects of e-MTB riding, from technical descents to endurance climbs.

Jessica's first stage was a combination of steep climbs and technical terrain. She was particularly impressed with how she needed to strategically manage the e-MTB's assistance modes to maintain battery life while maximizing performance. The camaraderie on the trail was palpable; riders encouraged each other, shared advice, and celebrated individual accomplishments.

As she crossed the finish line of the first stage, the sense of achievement was immense. Jessica realized that e-MTB racing required not only physical endurance and technical skills but also strategic thinking to balance the bike's battery use across demanding sections. Between stages, she attended workshops and social gatherings, deepening her understanding of e-MTB technology and its community.

One highlight of the event was a group ride organized by the race officials. This social ride provided an opportunity for participants to explore the local trails at a leisurely pace, exchanging stories and tips. Jessica found herself forming lasting connections with riders from different backgrounds, all united by their passion for e-MTB.

By the end of the Specialized eMTB Series event, Jessica's skills and confidence had grown exponentially. She finished the race with a respectable time and left with a newfound appreciation for the strategic elements of e-MTB riding. More importantly, she discovered a supportive and welcoming community that shared her love for adventure and innovation.

Inspired by her experience, Jessica continued to participate in other e-MTB events. She competed in the Enduro World Series (EWS-E), tackling international terrains and further honing her skills. Each race offered unique challenges and opportunities to learn, solidifying her place in the e-MTB racing scene.

Jessica's journey into e-MTB racing wasn't just about competing; it was about embracing a new facet of her passion for mountain biking, one that combined the thrill of traditional riding with the innovation of electric assistance. Through these events, she found not only personal growth and achievement but also a community that fueled her enthusiasm and supported her journey.

Her story is a testament to the vibrant world of e-MTB racing, where riders of all levels can find excitement, challenge, and camaraderie. Jessica's experience encourages others to explore the possibilities of e-MTB racing, proving that it's about more than competition—it's about connection, learning, and embracing the future of mountain biking.

Final Thoughts

e-MTB-specific events and races offer unique challenges and rewarding experiences for electric mountain biking enthusiasts. By participating in these events, you can test your skills, enjoy exhilarating trails, and connect with a dedicated community of e-MTB riders. Whether you aim to compete in international races or enjoy the festival atmosphere, there's an event tailored for every e-MTB rider. Embrace these opportunities to enhance your riding journey and create lasting memories. Chapter 10:

CHAPTER 49

Trail Maintenance and Advocacy

How can I support trail maintenance and advocacy efforts as an e-MTB rider?

Supporting trail maintenance and advocacy efforts is crucial for preserving and enhancing the trails we love to ride. By contributing to these efforts, e-MTB riders can help ensure that existing trails remain accessible and new trails that allow e-MTBs area created.

The easiest way we have found to learn about local groups is to stop by the local bike shops. They typically have handouts or other information on the shop bulletin board. Here's how you can get involved and make a difference in trail maintenance and advocacy. Here are some other ways you can get involved.

Join Local Trail Associations

Research Local Organizations

How to Use: Identify and join local trail or mountain biking associations that focus on trail maintenance and advocacy. Most already have lots of members that ride e-MTBs. If not, you can raise awareness about the benefits of e-MTBs.

Example: Lisa joined the "Mid-Atlantic Off-Road Enthusiasts (MORE)" to participate in their trail maintenance programs and advocacy efforts, including getting more trails opened for use by people riding Class 1 e-MTBs.

Participate in Meetings and Events

How to Use: Attend meetings, events, and workdays organized by these associations to stay informed and get involved.

Example: Mark regularly attends his local trail association's meetings and volunteer days, where he learns about trail projects, gets invited to group rides and contributes to maintenance efforts.

Volunteer for Trail Maintenance

Regular Maintenance Days

How to Use: Volunteer for trail maintenance days organized by local clubs, associations, or land management agencies.

Example: Sarah dedicates one weekend a month to volunteer with her local trail association, helping to clear debris, repair trails, and build new features.

Adopt-A-Trail Programs

How to Use: Participate in adopt-a-trail programs, where individuals or groups take responsibility for maintaining specific trail sections.

Example: Emma's riding club adopted a popular trail in their area, committing to regular maintenance and upkeep.

Trail Building Workshops

How to Use: Attend trail building workshops to learn proper techniques and contribute to new trail projects. This gives you an excellent opportunity to be sure that new trails allow e-MTBs

Example: David attended a trail building workshop organized by his local IMBA chapter, learning valuable skills and helping to build sustainable trails.

Financial Contributions

Donate to Trail Organizations

How to Use: Make financial contributions to trail associations and advocacy groups to support their work.

Example: Tom donates annually to the International Mountain Bicycling Association (IMBA), supporting their efforts to maintain and expand trail networks.

Fundraising Events

How to Use: Participate in or organize fundraising events to generate financial support for trail maintenance and advocacy.

Example: Lisa participated in a charity bike ride, raising funds to support local trail maintenance projects.

Advocacy and Public Engagement

Engage with Local Politicians

How to Use: Write to or meet with local representatives to advocate for trail access and funding for maintenance projects.

Example: Mark met with his city council members to discuss the importance of supporting local trail networks and securing funding for maintenance.

Public Awareness Campaigns

How to Use: Participate in or organize public awareness campaigns to educate the community about the importance of trail maintenance.

Example: Sarah helped create a social media campaign highlighting the benefits of well-maintained trails and encouraging community involvement.

Educate and Promote Trail Etiquette

Trail Use Education

How to Use: Educate fellow riders and trail users about proper trail etiquette to minimize impact and promote sustainable use.

Example: Emma shares trail etiquette tips with new riders during group rides, promoting respectful and responsible trail use.

Host Workshops and Clinics

How to Use: Organize or participate in workshops and clinics focused on sustainable riding practices and trail stewardship.

Example: David helped organize a clinic on sustainable riding techniques, teaching participants how to minimize trail impact.

Support Trail Stewardship Programs

Become a Trail Steward

How to Use: Enroll in trail stewardship programs that train and certify volunteers to oversee and maintain trails.

Example: Tom became a certified trail steward through his local trail association, regularly patrolling and maintaining trails in his area.

Encourage Responsible Use

How to Use: Advocate for and practice responsible trail use, encouraging others to do the same.

Example: Lisa encourages responsible trail use by setting a good example and educating her riding group on the importance of leaving no trace.

Community and Club Involvement

Join Biking Clubs

How to Use: Join biking clubs that emphasize community involvement and trail stewardship.

Example: Sarah's biking club regularly organizes trail maintenance days and advocacy events, supporting the local trail network.

Collaborate with Other Groups

How to Use: Collaborate with hiking, equestrian, and other outdoor recreation groups to promote shared stewardship of trails.

Examples: Sarah's biking club regularly organizes trail maintenance days and advocacy events, supporting the local trail network. Emma's biking club teamed up with a local hiking group to conduct a large-scale trail cleanup event, fostering community spirit and collaboration.

Detailed Examples of Trail Maintenance and Advocacy Efforts

Mountain Bike Hall of Fame (MBHOF)

Description: The MBHOF recognizes individuals and groups who have contributed significantly to the sport, including trail maintenance and advocacy.

How to Get Involved: Support the MBHOF by participating in their events, visiting the museum, and contributing to their initiatives.

Example: David attended the Hall of Fame induction ceremony, learning about pioneering trail builders and gaining inspiration for his own advocacy work.

Trailforks App and Website

Description: Trailforks is a comprehensive trail database and mapping tool that also supports trail maintenance and reporting.

How to Use: Use the app to report trail conditions, maintenance needs, and new trail construction. Contribute to the global trail database.

Example: Sarah uses Trailforks to report fallen trees and other trail obstructions, helping local trail managers address issues promptly.

Community Outreach and Education

Community Workshops

Description: Host or attend community workshops focused on sustainable trail use, maintenance techniques, and advocacy strategies.

How to Get Involved: Partner with local schools, community centers, and outdoor shops to organize educational workshops.

Example: Lisa co-organized a workshop at her local community center, where experts shared best practices for trail maintenance and sustainable riding techniques.

Public Awareness Campaigns

Description: Launch public awareness campaigns to educate the broader community about the benefits of trail stewardship and responsible riding.

How to Get Involved: Use social media, local news outlets, and community events to spread the message.

Example: Tom spearheaded a social media campaign celebrating Earth Day by highlighting local trail maintenance projects and encouraging community participation.

Participation in Multi-day Work Crews

Trail Building Vacations

Description: Participate in multi-day trail building vacations organized by trail associations or eco-tourism groups.

How to Get Involved: Sign up for these trips through organizations like IMBA or local trail clubs. You'll get the chance to work on major trail projects while exploring new locations.

Example: David joined an IMBA trail building vacation in Patagonia, working on new trail sections and enjoying some of the most scenic rides of his life.

Youth Engagement Programs

Description: Support or volunteer for youth engagement programs that educate young riders about trail maintenance and advocacy. These are typically multi-day programs held during the summer.

How to Get Involved: Partner with schools, youth groups, and biking clubs to organize programs and events.

Example: Sarah volunteered for a local youth biking camp, teaching kids the importance of trail stewardship and engaging them in hands-on maintenance activities. She felt great, especially after seeing a depressed teenage girl that had been assigned to her came alive after riding and connecting with nature. They have continued riding together regularly and she loves seeing how riding and being out in nature has smoothed out an otherwise difficult time in her teenage life.

Transforming Community Through Trail Advocacy

Mark, a dedicated e-MTB rider, took his passion for mountain biking to the next level by involving himself in trail advocacy and maintenance efforts. He joined his local IMBA chapter, participating in monthly trail workdays and attending community meetings to discuss trail access and conservation issues. Mark also became an advocate for sustainable trail use, educating new riders in his club about responsible riding practices. His efforts not only helped maintain the local trails but also fostered a strong, engaged community of riders dedicated to preserving and enhancing their riding environment. Best yet, all of the mountain biking trails in his community are now open to class one eMTBs.

Final Thoughts

Supporting trail maintenance and advocacy efforts is vital for sustaining and improving the trails we cherish. By joining local associations, volunteering for trail workdays, making financial contributions, engaging in public advocacy, and educating fellow riders, you can make a significant impact. These efforts ensure that our trail networks remain accessible, enjoyable, and sustainable for future generations of riders. Get involved, make a difference, and help foster a culture of responsibility and stewardship within the e-MTB community.

Now It is Time For You To Get Out There On Your Bike!

Congratulations! By embarking on this journey to master mountain biking, you've taken the first steps toward embracing a lifestyle filled with adventure, fitness, and community. This book aims to equip you with the knowledge and confidence to explore the trails, improve your skills, and enjoy the myriad benefits of mountain biking, whether on a traditional bike or an e-MTB.

It was our goal to get you started on the right foot as well as provide you an excellent reference moving into the future. Or example, we regularly reference the information in this book about essential tools for repairs and maintenance when we are loading up our bikes and gear for our many RV trips. It would be too easy to forget something otherwise. We hope we have succeeded and that you will give this book a glowing reference on whatever venue you purchased it on. Its also a great gift for young people leaving heading out for college or launching their own life.

Let's take a moment to reflect on what we've covered and look forward to how you can continue to grow and find joy in this incredible sport.

Reflecting on Your Progress

Getting Started

We began by addressing the fundamentals of mountain biking—essential gear, bike selection, and initial setup. Understanding the importance of starting with the right equipment laid a solid foundation for your journey. Like Jessica, who found the perfect trail bike through diligent research and professional fitting, you're now prepared to enjoy the trails comfortably and safely.

Skills Enhancement

Next, we delved into techniques for handling different terrains, from basic body positions to advanced skills for navigating rock gardens and mastering jumps. Learning these skills is akin to Tom's story, where practicing body positioning and braking techniques significantly improved his confidence and control on technical trails. Remember, mastering these techniques is a continuous process that will enhance over time with regular practice.

Maintenance and Repairs

Proper maintenance and the ability to perform basic repairs are crucial for any mountain biker. We covered how to keep your bike in top condition, troubleshoot common issues, and perform trail-side repairs. Like Sarah, who efficiently managed a mid-ride flat tire, you're now equipped to handle minor inconveniences and keep your rides smooth and uninterrupted.

Trail Selection and Navigation

Choosing the right trails and navigating them effectively were key topics we explored. With resources like Trailforks and local bike shops, you can find trails that match your skill level and preferences. Emma's story of exploring new trails with confidence and ensuring a safe ride by using GPS navigation can serve as inspiration for your own adventures.

Safety and Gear

We emphasized the importance of safety gear and preventative measures. Wearing the appropriate helmet, gloves, and pads, like Mark does on his rides, ensures you can tackle the trails with peace of mind. Understanding how to prevent injuries and knowing what to do in case of an accident are invaluable skills that will keep you safe and prepared.

Fitness and Training

Improving your physical performance through targeted exercises, tailored training plans, and proper nutrition were also integral parts of our discussion. For instance, Lisa's structured training routine improved her endurance and strength, enabling her to tackle longer and more challenging rides with confidence. By following similar fitness guidelines, you'll enhance your riding experience and overall health.

Community and Culture

Mountain biking is not just a sport; it's a community. We highlighted ways to connect with fellow riders, join local clubs, participate in events, and contribute to trail maintenance and advocacy. Jessica's involvement in women-specific clinics and local biking groups showed how fostering community ties can enrich your mountain biking journey. Building relationships and supporting the mountain biking community can bring fulfillment and camaraderie.

Advanced Topics

For those eager to delve deeper, we explored advanced skills, seasonal riding tips, women-specific advice, youth and family biking, first aid and safety, and traveling with your bike. Each section was designed to provide you with comprehensive knowledge and practical tips to enhance your biking experience. Whether you're planning a bikepacking adventure, teaching your kids to ride, or mastering winter biking, you're now equipped to enjoy the sport fully and safely.

Embracing the Journey

Mountain biking is a lifelong journey filled with exploration, learning, and growth. Each ride is an opportunity to challenge yourself, connect with nature, and experience the thrill of conquering new trails. Let the stories and lessons shared in this book inspire and guide you as you continue to advance your skills and deepen your passion for mountain biking.

Real-Life Inspirations

Consider Jessica's journey. From a novice rider to an avid e-MTB racer, she embraced every challenge, learned from each experience, and built meaningful connections within the community. Her story illustrates the transformative power of mountain biking—not just as a physical activity, but as a vehicle for personal growth and community building.

Mark's dedication to safety and preparedness serves as a reminder of the importance of being well-equipped and informed. His proactive approach to maintenance and first aid ensured he could handle any situation, allowing him to ride confidently and safely.

Lisa's commitment to training and fitness highlights the benefits of a structured approach to physical preparation. By following a tailored training program, she improved her endurance and performance, making her rides more enjoyable and less exhausting.

Your Path Forward

Now that you've armed yourself with the knowledge and tips shared in this book, it's time to hit the trails with confidence. Here are some actionable steps to keep you motivated and on the path to mastery:

Set Goals

Define clear, attainable goals for your mountain biking journey. Whether it's mastering a specific trail, improving your technical skills, or participating in an e-MTB race, having goals will keep you focused and motivated.

Join a Community

Connect with local biking groups or online forums. Engage with fellow riders, share experiences, and participate in group rides or events.

Continue Learning

Keep honing your skills through regular practice, attending clinics, and seeking feedback from experienced riders. The learning never stops in mountain biking.

Stay Prepared

Equip yourself with the right gear, maintain your bike regularly, and carry essential tools and first aid kit on every ride.

Explore New Trails

Venture out to new trails and locations. Each new trail presents unique challenges and opportunities to grow as a rider.

Advocate and Volunteer

Get involved in trail maintenance and advocacy efforts. Supporting trail sustainability ensures future generations can enjoy the sport.

Final, Final, Thoughts

Mountain biking brings together the thrill of adventure, the beauty of nature, and the joy of community. It's a sport that challenges the body, mind, and spirit, offering endless opportunities for growth and discovery. As you continue on your journey, remember that every ride is a chance to learn, connect, and enjoy the incredible experiences that mountain biking offers.

Embrace the ride, savor each moment on the trail, and let the knowledge and inspiration from this book guide you to new heights. Whether you're a seasoned rider or just starting, the world of mountain biking is yours to explore. So gear up, hit the trails, and discover the endless possibilities that await you.

Happy riding!

About the Author

I've always loved bikes. My earliest memories involve riding my bike all around town—to school, baseball practice, soccer, the pool, and to friends' houses. I rode at least ten, but often twenty miles a day, getting where I needed to go. And none of it was easy or flat—plus, I only had a single speed bike for most of my childhood.

When I turned 16, I couldn't wait to get a car, but once I had one, I missed riding a bike. So, I got my first mountain bike. This was in the late 1980s, a time when there was no suspension—just robust frames that could withstand jumps and crashes.

I had a lot of fun on that bike. When front forks came out, I upgraded, and the trails felt so much smoother! I envied my friend who had a full suspension Cannondale, thanks to his generous parents. It pogoed uphill but was super fast downhill. I finally got my first full suspension bike in the late 1990s after receiving a bonus at work. That GT-LTS 1 was heavy but climbed like a dream, soaking up all the bumps. I rode about 50 miles every weekend.

Over time, I owned many bikes, always amazed at how designers made them lighter and better. Disk brakes were a revelation, a significant improvement over the old V-style and cantilever rim brakes that used to make my hands and forearms sore on long rides.

After getting married and having kids, I bought used bikes for everyone. We started with run-bikes, then moved to mountain bikes with tiny wheels. The wheels grew in size as the kids grew until finally, everyone had adult-sized bikes. While they grew up, we took the kids biking at least once a week, often going on family adventures in the woods. With four kids, keeping everyone's tires full of air and brakes working was no joke, but we developed an assembly line method to get everyone ready. Six bikes? Check! Six hydration packs? Check! Six helmets? Check! Looking back, I'm not sure how we managed it all, but the kids loved to ride, so it was worth it.

Due to injuries, you'll usually see me riding an electric assist mountain bike now. It allows me to continue going on long, challenging rides and exploring new places. My downhill and cross-country bikes spend most of their time in the garage.

In recent years, I've spent months on the road with my cargo e-bike and e-MTB, traveling in an RV equipped with all my bike gear, the X-pen for the dog, and a couple of inflatable paddle boards. We've traveled all over the country, usually staying at state parks. Every few days, we stay at a campground with electricity to charge our bikes. We also stay near water for paddle boarding with great bike trails close by.

Now that my kids are grown, I decided to write this book to share everything I know about mountain biking. If I can inspire just a few people to try mountain biking and fall in love with it, or help a few riders improve their skills and take on bigger challenges, I'll consider that a huge win.

This book aims to equip you with the knowledge and confidence to explore trails, improve your skills, and enjoy the myriad benefits of mountain biking, whether on a traditional bike or an e-MTB. Bookmark the chapters on bike maintenance, gear checklists, epic places to ride, traveling with your bike, and specialized tools. I hope you find them as helpful and inspiring as I do.

Best yet, I hope to see you out on the trail someday!

J.J. Quest

Please Tell Us What You Think

Dear Mountain Biking Enthusiast,

Thank you for choosing "Mastering Mountain Biking"! We've packed this book with everything you need to conquer trails and elevate your mountain biking experience.

Your journey with us doesn't end here. We'd love to hear how this book has impacted your rides and adventures. By sharing your thoughts, you'll not only help fellow bikers but also inspire more people to embrace the thrill of mountain biking.

Please take a moment to scan the QR code below or use the link and leave us a review. Your feedback is invaluable to us and to all eager riders looking to hit the trails with confidence.

https://amzn.to/4egi1E1

Happy trails and ride on!

Warm regards,

J. J. Quest

Thank You for Your Support

Hope to see you out on the trail!

Printed in Dunstable, United Kingdom